Freshman Year Experience Plan for Success

Third Edition

Edited by

Eva Brickman
Deborah Thinnes
Barbara Osmon

Purdue University Calumet

Kendall Hunt
p u b l i s h i n g   c o m p a n y
4050 Westmark Drive • P O Box 1840 • Dubuque IA 52004-1840

Contents

Chancellor's Message

Welcome to Purdue University Calumet!

Congratulations on your decision to pursue an internationally respected Purdue degree at Purdue Calumet.

As part of the Purdue University system, Purdue Calumet offers the high quality education reflective of the Purdue reputation. Purdue Calumet graduates work as NASA engineers, physicians, family therapists, computing technologists, broadcast and print journalists, business and industrial executives, and much more.

Our most successful Purdue Calumet students—and graduates—are committed, ambitious and motivated individuals who come to our campus with a plan for success. You, too, undoubtedly, have a plan to earn a Purdue degree and apply it in ways that enrich your life and benefit the rest of our society.

Please understand that whatever your plan for success is, Purdue Calumet will help you make it a reality. Through our programs and services, such as new student orientation, freshman seminars, advising, mentoring, and supplemental instruction; through contact with faculty members who take an interest in your learning; and through our engaging campus environment, you will experience Purdue Calumet as a partner in your education.

Purdue Calumet is ready to help you prepare for the rest of your life. You have my best wishes for this exciting adventure.

Sincerely,

Howard Cohen
Chancellor

Chapter 1

Expectations and Challenges

Surely there is a mine for silver, and a place for gold which they refine . . .
But where shall wisdom be found?

—The Book of Job

WHAT DOES IT MEAN TO HAVE A COLLEGE EDUCATION?

When asked what college means to them, students say such things as it's:

" . . . a means to a better job."

" . . . something to do instead of working."

" . . . my parents' dream for me."

" . . . something that comes after high school."

" . . . a place to learn."

" . . . a place to be irresponsible and have fun."

While a college experience may be any or all of the above for a student, a college education is not a product nor a "thing" one gets; it is a process one participates in. A college education:

- Is an exposure to a life and a way of looking at the world through many new and different lenses.
- Can provide a better understanding of the world in which we live and increase our ability for meaningful interactions within our environments.
- Expands and deepens an increasing awareness of our creativity.
- Provides an opportunity to grow in compassion and understanding of other people, to gain a new appreciation of differences, and to obtain a new sense of responsibility for our life.
- Helps develop effective problem solving skills and strategies that equip us for various employment, cultural, and interpersonal opportunities.

The comedian Woody Allen is reported to have said that 80% of success in life simply comes from "showing up." Unfortunately "showing up" is not enough to guarantee success in college. It's what a student chooses "to do" after "showing up" that makes the difference. College furnishes the environment and the opportunities for success. The task for every student is to decide whether or not to take advantage of those opportunities. Attending class, completing assignments, interacting with professors, passing tests, and being involved in extracurricular activities are important parts of your years in college. Equally important are the decisions made, the goals set, and the relationships formed. In sum, what a college experience means depends on what one chooses to do now that they have shown up.

> *Now, here, you see, it takes all the running you can do to keep in the same place. If you want to get somewhere else, you must run twice as fast as that.*
> —Lewis Carroll
> *Through the Looking-Glass*

Realizing that the freshman year is a challenging time, your college provides a wealth of resources to help its new students with the transition. This text details a number of transition issues and changes you will encounter. Read carefully and think about the transition and what it means to you. There are clubs and organizations covering special interest groups, service clubs, religious groups, recreational clubs, and scholastic organizations.

New students are encouraged to join clubs and participate in campus activities. Campus involvement is one way of making a connection with the larger student body. A word of caution: balance in life is an important ingredient of success. A careful examination of personal goals and use of time gives one a fairly good idea of how to balance the time between studies, work, and extracurricular activities.

WHAT IS EXPECTED OF NEW STUDENTS?

If the extent of personal freedom in college is an eye-opening experience for new students, an equally important element of the transition equation is the personal responsibility that accompanies the new freedom. It is important to maintain personal and academic freedom and maximize individual responsibility.

> *The freedom from work, from restraint, from accountability, wondrous in its inception, became banal and counterfeit. Without rules there was no way to say no, and worse, no way to say yes.*
> —Thomas Farber

As a new student, you become a part of an exciting new community on campus. As a member of the community, you are expected to be treated and treat other members of this community with honesty, courtesy, tolerance, and respect. It has been said that a well-educated person can disagree without being disagreeable. A valuable part of your experience will be getting to know people with very different values and backgrounds from your own; your ability to treat them with respect and to engage in meaningful discourse will enhance your life and theirs.

In all of your communications, whether they are in person, in writing, or electronic, avoid vulgarity, profanity, and other offensive content. Any remarks or acts that may be interpreted as sexist, racist, or discriminatory against certain groups are prohibited.

New students are expected to assume responsibility for their education and behavior. Among those expectations are the following:

Classroom conduct. Appropriate classroom conduct is expected of all students. Students should arrive at class on time and be prepared with the necessary books, notes, paper, and writing supplies. Coming prepared to class also means having completed assigned readings, reviewed notes, and prepared questions.

Working on homework from another course, carrying on side conversations, and chatter during a lecture are not appropriate.

Cultivating relationships with faculty is important. Develop the interpersonal skills that promote interaction with professors and instructors. The first step is to find out what they expect of students and what students can expect from them. This information is usually found in the course syllabus and/or is discussed on the first day of class. Generally speaking, most professors expect students to:

- *Attend class regularly.* You lose when you skip a class. If you must miss a class, arrange for another student to keep notes for you (don't expect the professors to give you theirs). Make sure you get any assignments that were announced.
- *Accept responsibility.* Don't make excuses; accept responsibility for your own learning.
- *Submit high-quality work in both content and form.* Do the best you can in quality and neatness. Some instructors accept only typed papers, and students without personal computers should take advantage of the campus computer labs.
- *Turn assignments in on time.* Late assignments suggest a lack of enthusiasm and commitment. Habitually handing assignments in late is a bad habit that employers are less forgiving of.
- *Arrive on time and be attentive in class.* Late arrivals are a distraction to the entire class. If you must be late, find the nearest convenient seat and quickly and quietly sit down.
- *Participate in class discussions.* Participation in class is valued by some professors and not encouraged by others. Follow the preferences for each professor.
- *Meet with professors outside of class.* A good way to get to know your professor is to prepare some questions based on previous classes, readings, and your own reflections that you can ask the professor before or after class, or in his/her office.

Academic honesty. Faculty and staff expect students and faculty alike to maintain the highest standards of academic honesty. Academic dishonesty includes but is not limited to:

- Stealing a copy of the exam ahead of time
- Copying from someone else's paper
- Sending or receiving signals during an exam
- Using unauthorized notes during an exam
- Taking an exam for another student
- Letting another student take an exam for you
- Handing in a paper that you have not written

Plagiarism is a specific form of cheating in which a student fails to give proper credit for written work that belongs to someone else. It is trying to pass off the work of others as one's own. Students falsely assume that they will not be caught; however, professors are very adept at identifying work that has been incorrectly documented or "borrowed" from another source without proper citation. Also, new technology has been developed to compare a student's papers with other students' work and papers collected from sources like the Internet, journals, books or other publications. Knowingly representing the words or ideas of another as your own in any academic exercise or activity carries with it serious consequences.

DEVELOPMENTAL CHANGES

When we plant a rose seed in the earth, we notice that it is small, but we do not criticize it as "rootless and stemless." We treat it as a seed, giving it the water and nourishment required of a seed. When it first shoots up out of the earth, we don't condemn it as immature and underdeveloped; nor do we criticize the buds for not being open when they appear. We stand in wonder at the process taking place and give the plant the care it needs at each stage of its development. The rose is a rose from the time it is a seed to the time it dies. Within it, at all times, it contains its whole potential. It seems to be constantly in the process of change; yet at each stage, at each moment, it is perfectly all right as it is.

—W. Timothy Gallwey
The Inner Game of Tennis

You can expect to go through a great number of changes during your college years. Most of these changes will not be noticeable to the naked eye because they take place inside of you. How you cope with these changes will be determined mainly by your personality, your past experience, and your current life situation. Many students glide right through this time of transition with little awareness that anything new has occurred. Others come through thrashing and kicking. Regardless, the one thing you can count on is that you will grow and change during the next few years.

As you begin to explore your personal values and set goals for your future, you will be creating a world view that is unique to you. This is good, and this is healthy. It is important to realize that there are some very normal developmental tasks which you will be completing during the next few years.

One of the most challenging tasks is redefining relationships with your family. The important thing to remember is that these next years will be a period of adjustment for you and your family. Your first trip home may start out as a hero's welcome and end in tears and disagreement. Be patient! Don't try to flex all of your new freedom at once. Give your family a chance to get used to the new you. And remember, your family hasn't been standing still while you have been gone. They may have changed and grown as well. Finding your new place within the family may take patience and time.

There is no way to predict how you will move through these next four years. To be sure, at times you will find yourself struggling and feeling out of sorts. At other times, life will seem wonderful, and you will be on top of the world. The important thing to remember is that normal developmental changes will take place. The college years are a time of change and, while you may not always be at ease as those changes unfold, you are OKAY!

ELEMENTS OF SUCCESS

Success in all of its forms and varieties is a goal of every student. However, wanting to succeed and doing what is necessary to succeed are two very different things. This section details suggestions and ideas about how to bridge the gap between desiring and actually achieving success. We encourage you to read and make use of the ideas presented, because they are only as helpful as you make them. There are no quick fixes, no easy answers.

The first step in succeeding at something is realizing that wanting to succeed is just the starting place. Additional factors in any successful college experience include: (1) attitude about school and life; (2) prior academic experience and ability; (3) ability to effectively manage time and to discipline one's self; (4) ability to relate to and get along with others; and (5) the learning environment.

> *Two roads diverged in a wood and I took the one less traveled by,*
> *and that has made all the difference.*
> —ROBERT FROST
> *THE ROAD NOT TAKEN*

Attitude. Attitude is a combination of thoughts and feelings. Much of a student's attitude about college is determined by how and why he/she chose to be here and how he/she feels about that choice. Some students find themselves in college, but are not aware how they arrived at the decision to attend. Do you want to be here? Are you in school because someone said you had to come? Enrolling in college because someone else said you should, may motivate you to enroll, but won't necessarily enable you to succeed. In order to succeed, you need to have your own reasons for attending; you need to "own" the decision to come to school.

There are many different (but no right) reasons for attending college. Some students pursue a degree in order to get a good job or to advance into a higher position in their current job. Others come to school for social reasons—high school was fun, so college will be even more fun! Some would rather go to school than work full-time. Others find it an easy way to move away from home and have their parents or others pay for it! Some students decide on a college education because they love learning and see college as an opportunity to pursue that love.

The reasons for choosing to go to college are as limitless as the persons attending. Reasons for attending also change over time as events and circumstances unfold. Be reflective; visit with yourself from time to time about why you are in college. Are those reasons being fulfilled? What are you doing to fulfill them?

The thing to remember is that, when the days are long and the nights are short, your attitude about school will determine how hard you are willing to work to make it work!

Experience and ability. Prior academic experience and ability play an important role in your success. Students who arrive at college with a strong academic background have an advantage. New ideas are more quickly assimilated when they can be associated with prior knowledge. Don't rest on your laurels however; professors expect a lot.

This is not to say that a lack of prior strong academic experience prohibits success, but it will take greater commitment and hard work to catch on in some of your classes. It is also a fairly common experience for "average" high school students to "catch fire" in the stimulating environment of college.

Prior academic experience includes a knowledge of basic learning and life skills. Do you know how to study, how to manage time, how to set goals, and how to communicate effectively? Many students come to college unaware of the need for these skills. They register for classes, buy their books, attend the first day of class, and begin to "study." They are quickly disillusioned with college and their own abilities, as the old habits that worked in high school don't seem to be working now, as the work piles higher and higher, and as the probability of success sinks lower and lower.

Success is not a matter of studying more or studying harder, it is a matter of studying smarter. An average student in high school will probably need to work harder and smarter to be an average student in college. College is definitely more difficult than high school, and success in high school does not necessarily ensure success in college. Taking the time to learn some study strategies that are applicable in all of your classes is time well spent.

We challenge you to examine and reflect on your values and your goals and the strategies you need to develop as school begins. Principles and strategies that are helpful in learning how to successfully juggle the demands of college, work, family, friends, and extracurricular activities are described herein. Discover how learning takes place and how you can best structure your own learning experiences to promote success.

Experiences are dynamic. Periodically take the time to stop and reflect on yours. What's going right? Wrong? What can you do to sustain or alter the experiences you are having at college?

Self-discipline. Self-discipline and effective time management are vital keys to success. Students who are self-disciplined are better able to handle the increased freedom that comes with college. One of the first things that is discovered about college life is that in many classes attendance is not required. Unfortunately, some students interpret this to mean that attendance is not important. Nothing can be farther from the truth. Skipping class is a poor strategy for achieving success. Having decided to enroll in college, and after having paid the tuition, deciding not to attend class is counter-productive and costly!

Interpersonal skills. Another very important part of success at any college is the ability to relate to and get along with other people. This includes roommates, friends, other students, faculty, and family. Although satisfactory progress towards a degree is measured in grades, the sense of well-being and accomplishment may well be measured by the ability to make friends, relate to classmates, and interact with faculty.

Having significant people who support you in your decision to attend college is a big help in your success. These are the people who remind you of your commitment and encourage you to continue on with your plans when you are tired and discouraged. They are the same people who share in your accomplishments and your success. These people comprise an important part of your support network. Although they cannot make you succeed, they can remind you of your goals and even help lighten some of the burden you carry. Recognize their support. "Good strokes for good folks" goes a long way to ensuring their continued support.

Environment. Finally, success in college is determined by the learning environment, which includes defining and setting up an area for studying. By following a few basic suggestions, a supportive study environment can be created. Study in the same place at the same time and use a signal to tell roommates and yourself that you are studying.

This book is a practical aid to understanding and developing the strategies necessary to make satisfactory progress as a college student. The rate of progress (time it takes) and the qualitative measurement of that progress (grades received) are determined by individual circumstances. Understanding the factors that impact on that success—attitude, prior academic experience, self-discipline, relations with others, and the working/studying environment—helps to bridge the gap between wanting success and achieving success.

Chapter 2

Prioritizing Your Time to Match Your Goals

CASE STUDY

Sam's Saturday

Sam had planned to finish all his homework on Saturday afternoon and had figured out how much time he would need to spend on each of his English, math, sociology, and physical geography classes. He needed to complete everything by 6:00 p.m., as he had a date that night. He wanted to get in his daily workout before starting the study session, so he planned to put in an hour at the fitness center from 11:00-12:00, catch some lunch, and then hit the books. He had 20 math problems to complete, had to read a chapter in sociology, needed to finish writing his English paper, and had to write up his lab report for geography class. The English paper would take the most time and concentration, followed by the difficult math problems. He didn't expect the lab report to take much time, and thought that reading the sociology chapter would be a breeze.

While at the fitness center, he realized that he needed to get gas and clean up the car for that evening, so he decided to take care of that before going home. At the gas station, he ran into a friend he hadn't seen for awhile. In the course of their conversation, the friend told Sam he didn't like the movie Sam and his date were planning to see. They spent 20 minutes talking, and Sam still needed to get the car washed. There was a line at the car wash, a line at the drive through, and a line at the ATM, none of which he anticipated, and he had now wasted 90 minutes.

When Sam got home, his mother asked him to keep an eye on his little sister and her friend who were out rollerblading. He told his Mom he had to study, but she promised she'd only be gone for an hour. He started reading his sociology chapter because that was the easiest. His mind started to wander, and he thought he'd better call his date to see if she'd rather see a different movie. Once he got on the phone, they talked longer than expected, and by the time he got back on track, it was already 3:00 p.m.

Since he couldn't concentrate on the reading, Sam decided to start working some math problems. Halfway through them, he heard his sister crying hysterically from outside. He yelled for his Mom, but she hadn't returned, so he had to go check what was wrong with his sister. She had fallen and scraped her knees badly, and she was really freaked with the blood. He had to clean and bandage her cut, and then got her a snack to calm her down. He told her to stay inside so he could get his homework done.

Sam started working on his lab report; some of the information his lab partner should have included was missing. He was really annoyed with his lab partner and felt frustrated that he was spending time on a class that doesn't apply to his major. While still fuming about this class, his Dad walked in saying, "I thought you were going to mow the lawn today." When Sam tried to explain that he'd been studying all afternoon, he had to listen to another one of those "you-need-to-take-more-responsibility-around-the-house" lectures.

It's now after 5:00 p.m. Sam hasn't completed one full assignment, and he needs to shower and change before going out.

Reflections

- Why did Sam's study plans fail?
- What could Sam have done differently to ensure that he accomplished his goals?
- What time management strategies could have helped Sam?

INTRODUCTION

Using our time wisely is as important as using our money wisely. Like money, time is something you can only spend once. When it is gone, you can't get it back. Fortunately, we receive a new supply of time every day, but unlike money, it can't be stored or accumulated. It must be spent each day. What you get in return for your time is up to you.

In this chapter we will take a look at ways to control the use of time. You will be asked to examine how you currently spend time. We will explore how our goals should form the foundation for the way we "budget," or plan to use time. Once you have established your goals, there are three scheduling tools that will help you get organized. They are the *weekly schedule,* the *semester schedule,* and the *daily to-do list.* Common time management problems such as *procrastination* and *distractions* will be discussed, and suggestions will be given on how to avoid these problems. We hope that you will learn to make the best use of your time while you are in college. It's an investment for life.

Pretest

Before we begin to talk about time, let's get a clear idea of how you currently use your time. There are a total of 168 hours in every week. How are you using those hours? Keep track of a "normal week" in your life. There are probably some routine things that you do every day that take about the same amount of time. You can multiply the average daily minutes/hours spent doing each of these activities by seven days to see how much time is spent per week. There might also be things that you do only once or twice a week. Make a note of them and approximate how many hours they involve. In the space provided below, write the number of hours per week that you spend on each of the following activities:

_____ Sleeping

_____ Eating/preparing meals/clean-up

_____ Bathing/dressing/grooming/etc.

_____ Commuting/traveling to and from work, the college, etc.

_____ Working

_____ Attending class

_____ Doing homework

_____ Socializing/hanging out with friends

_____ Talking on the phone

_____ Doing chores/housework/laundry/etc.

_____ Running errands

_____ Watching television

_____ Using the computer

_____ Athletics/clubs/other activities

_____ Church/religious activities

_____ Family activities and events

_____ Exercising/working out

_____ Shopping

_____ Hobbies

_____ Other _____

_____ Other _____

_____ Other _____

_____ Total

Subtract the total number from 168. How many hours do you have left? Can you fit a study schedule into your week?

MAKING TIME FOR COLLEGE

Learning how to structure time is one of the biggest adjustments many college students have to make. Most college classes don't meet every day. Unlike high school, you might not have a "regular" schedule. You may be taking a late starting class that begins two weeks after the semester is underway or a combination of day, twilight, and evening classes. Some courses require assignments that must be completed in a lab or that require a significant amount of reading or research beyond what is covered in the textbook. Don't expect your instructors to give you class time to do homework. It is your responsibility to spend time out of class doing assignments and studying for tests.

Remember this rule of thumb: "For every hour of class time, you should expect to spend at least two hours outside of class doing independent work." For homework-intensive courses such as accounting and mathematics, you may need as much as four hours of study time per class hour. That's why you are considered a full-time student when you are taking 12 or more credit hours of coursework. Twelve hours of class time per week plus 24 hours of studying equals a 36-hour time commitment. If you are enrolled in 15 credit hours of coursework, you have made a 45-hour per week commitment. This can become a problem if you were not prepared to devote that much time to college. Most of you have other factors, sometimes called "having a life," that impact the amount of time you devote to your education.

Alternative instructional formats may also lead students to underestimate the study time needed for a class. Some students deliberately choose telecourses, blended courses (combination of half class attendance and half on-line instruction), or total on-line courses. They think that the demands in such classes will be less than in a traditional course meeting 3–5 hours per week. In fact, the opposite is true. Successful performance in these classes may require a significant additional time commitment. These courses also require that students be motivated, independent learners.

Working Students

In addition to attending classes, many college students work 20 hours per week or more. Generally, if you are a full-time student, you should limit your work hours. If you must work full time, it would be better to attend college as a part-time student. People who try to take on too much often end up getting worse grades, failing, or dropping courses. Although it may seem that it will take you much longer to complete your degree if you take the minimum course load each semester, it will be faster and less expensive to take only the amount of coursework you can realistically accomplish. Dropping, failing, and having to repeat classes ends up costing you more time and money in the long run.

Trying to get a schedule that balances work and classes can be difficult. If your job is entry level and not significant to your career path, you may want to consider finding an on-campus job. Colleges employ many students in a wide variety of positions. Your work hours can often be scheduled around your classes. Although work-study jobs are tied to financial aid eligibility, other student jobs are funded through the college budget. Most departments have student workers who answer phones, make photocopies, assist with mailings, and do other light office work. Computer lab assistants, library aides, childcare attendants, tutors, bookstore clerks, grounds workers, and campus escorts are other job possibilities. One of the benefits of working at the college is your employer's commitment to helping you succeed as a student. To see a list of job openings and to apply for a student worker position, check with your college's placement center or office of career services.

Other Demands on Your Time

Those of you who are not traditional-aged college students probably have many life roles in addition to that of student. You may be married and/or have children to support and/or be a caregiver for ailing or elderly parents. You may be responsible for running a household and do most of the chores such as grocery shopping, cooking, cleaning, laundry, yard work, home maintenance and repairs, chauffeuring others back and forth to activities/events, etc. Even those of you who are in the 18-to-21-year-old age group probably have significant demands on your time in addition to classes, homework, and a job. Learning how to prioritize your time to do the things that are most important is one of the most valuable skills you can develop.

SETTING YOUR GOALS

Your Personal Life Mission

Before you devote time to any activity, you should think about how it fits into your life, and whether it helps you accomplish any of your goals. If you don't know what your goals are, now is the time to give thoughtful consideration to what you want to do with your life. In his book, *The Seven Habits of Highly Effective People* (highly recommended reading), Dr. Stephen Covey discusses finding your purpose in life and writing a personal mission statement. Knowing what you want from your life will help you evaluate how to invest your time. Once you have decided what is important, it's time to set some goals.

How to Get Started

When asked to state their goals, many people can only generate one or two vague wishes or dreams. To be a successful college student, you need to move beyond the dream stage and set goals that will be the basis for action. A goal should be your destination or end point. It should be specific and measurable enough that you will know when you've achieved it. For example, counselors have had countless students tell them that their goal in life is to be happy. That's nice, but what are you going to do to get happiness? How will you know when you've achieved ultimate happiness? When you get there, can you stop pursuing happiness? Maybe happiness isn't the goal. Maybe happiness is a consequence or byproduct—something you get from achieving your real goals.

Let's consider some basic criteria for a well-written goal statement:

1. It needs to be **specific.** You need to know exactly what it is you plan to accomplish. Example: *I will earn a Bachelor of Arts degree.*

2. It needs to be **realistic.** Your goal has to be something you can actually accomplish; otherwise you will just frustrate and discourage yourself. Also, you must *believe* that you can achieve your goal in order for it to be realistic.

3. It needs to be **for yourself and within your control.** You can only set goals for one person—you. You cannot control other people's thoughts or actions. Even if it is your parents' fondest wish that you graduate from college, it will only happen if you decide to make it happen. They can encourage you, but earning your degree must be *your* goal.

4. It needs to be **measurable.** You will want to know when you're there so you can stop pursuing that one and move on to your next goal. You also need to identify the costs involved. Everything you will want to accomplish has a cost. Sometimes it is money. Most often the cost is time and effort. Sometimes it is giving up something to get something else.

Taking the example of getting a degree, your goal statement might read: *"I want to earn a Bachelor of Arts degree from my college in 4 years by taking 12–15 credit hours per semester. The costs involved will be money for tuition, fees, books and transportation, plus 30 hours per week of study time to maintain a 3.0 GPA."*

This goal statement is right on target, reflecting all of our criteria. We already said that it is specific and within your control. Completing the requirements for a Bachelor of Arts degree in four years is a realistic time frame if you are taking the minimum full-time course load each semester and have some required developmental courses as prerequisites. It is measurable; you will receive a diploma when you are done. It identifies the major costs, although you may have other costs such as childcare, reduced income because of reduced work hours, or agreeing to live at home in order to save money.

Long- and Short-Term Goals

You can set goals for any part of your life. You might have personal goals, career goals, family goals, spiritual goals, educational goals, and so forth. They can be very short term (as in things you want to accomplish this week or this semester), or they may be long range and stretch far into your future. Once you have learned to be specific, realistic, and determine how to measure, it is easier to develop a plan of action based on your goals. When you have some long-term goals, you can set several short-term goals that are actually the steps in your action plan. Think of something right now that you want for yourself in the next five years. Write it down here:

_____

Check to see that it fits the criteria for a well-written goal statement. Now, think about what you have to do to be halfway toward achieving your goal. Write that step down:

_____

Keep breaking each new goal in half until you can clearly see the starting point or first step. Reorganize your list in "start-to-finish" order and you will have a great action plan ready to implement. That's the purpose of a goal, to move you into action.

MANAGING YOUR TIME

Do you ever feel like a hamster on a wheel, always running, but never really getting anywhere? You're constantly busy, but never accomplish everything you need to do? When people talk about managing time, what they really mean is managing your activities to make the best use of your time. Think about this for a moment: How you spend your time is a direct reflection of your priorities. Is that true for you? Or are you giving priority to things that you don't truly value? Do you allow low priority activities to use up time that could be spent doing better things? If so, you need to make a lifestyle change. Begin to make conscious choices about how you invest your time. By setting goals and systematically working toward achieving them, you will find that your life will have more purpose and meaning. You will accomplish more. We all have the same number of hours each day. The difference between people who are productive and those who seem to drift along not getting much done is the way they view and use those hours.

The Use of Scheduling Tools

Most people need some visual aids to help them plan how to use their time. It's too hard to remember everything, especially now that you've added homework to your already busy life. It's not necessary to have a Palm Pilot to keep track of your life. Writing things down can be just as effective. There are many wonderful organizational notebooks and planners on the market, and finding something practical to use should not be difficult or expensive. The three major tools that work for most people are a weekly schedule, a semester schedule, and a daily "to-do" list.

The **semester schedule** allows you to see everything at once. We like the month-at-a-glance type calendars, although some people prefer the big poster-sized calendars that show several months (or even the whole year) on one page. Choose whichever seems right for you, and start to fill in known deadlines and future activities: a family wedding coming up next month, your psychology paper due 3 weeks before the end of the semester, your midterm exams, the church bazaar you volunteered to help with, the neighborhood watch meeting and potluck, your six-month dental check-up, and everything else you've made a commitment to do. Putting all of these down on a calendar helps you see in advance what you have to do so you aren't "surprised" by a deadline you forgot. If you are a parent with children who are involved in a variety of activities, you have probably already discovered the value of a centrally-located calendar that becomes the family's master schedule.

A **weekly schedule** is the cornerstone of your time/activity management plan. It is an outline that allows you to see how your time is budgeted. The chart at the end of this chapter that you will use for the homework assignment is a typical weekly schedule form. Make copies to use if your schedule changes from week to week. Start by filling in your fixed time commitments. These are things like your classes, work hours, time spent commuting, eating, grooming, sleeping, study time, and anything else you do regularly every week. If you go to temple, mosque, or church every week, put that on your schedule. If you have band practice every Monday evening, a club meeting on Thursdays, or family dinner on Sunday afternoons, include these activities. Be sure to write in study sessions for your classes. Set aside specific hours each week to do your homework and study—don't just hope you have time left over after all of your other activities are done. When you have finished filling in your fixed time commitments, you will easily see where you have discretionary time. We'll talk about how to use that to your best advantage a little later.

Your daily **to-do list** can be your best ally in your effort to control how you use your time. After consulting your weekly schedule and semester (or monthly) calendar to see what you are committed to doing, make a list of the things you need and want to accomplish that day. Most of the things we do fall into one of three categories:

1.   *Responsibilities*—These are things you have to do. Taking care of yourself (personal hygiene, getting enough sleep, eating, exercising, etc.), taking care of your dependents, and taking care of the things you own all fall into this category. Your job, if you are employed, and your education are key parts of your responsibilities. Some of your responsibilities are inescapable. You must devote whatever time is

necessary to take care of them. Other responsibilities can be reduced. For example, owning high maintenance items that require a lot of care and/or attention may not be worth your time at this point in your life. Most of your normal responsibilities should be predictable enough to include on your weekly or monthly schedule. You should budget an adequate amount of time to fulfill your responsibilities.

2. *Urgent*—These are activities that require immediate attention. Sometimes emergencies happen, and there is nothing you can do about it except drop everything and handle them. Urgent activities are often unplanned, and they typically go to the top of your to-do list. However, there is one type of urgent activity over which you can exert some control: things that you have put off until they become crises/emergencies. If you typically wait until the night before a big assignment is due and then rush around frantically trying to complete it, you need to change this very bad and stressful habit.

3. *Discretionary*—Activities you want to do for yourself that don't have a specific deadline fall into this category. You don't have to do them, but you want to do them. They're like the luxury items in your financial budget. They're "wants" rather than "needs." You should make time in your life for a healthy dose of relaxation. It is important to keep a balance of discretionary activities—not too much, not too little.

Now, go back to your to-do list. Prioritize the items you listed. Use colors, numbers, or some other system to show whether this activity is something you must get done today at all costs, something that should be taken care of today, or something that could be done later if it doesn't get done today. Re-order your list so the "must-do" items are at the top, followed by the "should-do" activities. The "want-to-do" items can go to the bottom of the list. If you take 10 to 15 minutes each day to plan and organize, you will find that you are much more productive. The things you most need/want to accomplish, you will do first. Checking completed tasks off the list is very rewarding for some people and reinforces their feelings of accomplishment.

Evaluate your weekly schedule in the same way you looked at your to-do list. You should have filled in the things that you consider major responsibilities. This is the part that correlates with your goals. For example, one semester a student complained to his instructor that attending her class was interfering with his job working in a local warehouse. He was faced with two choices: he could quit his job, or he could drop/fail the class. If his main goal was to keep the warehouse job, then he needed to drop the class. Assuming that attending college was one of his life goals, he needed to register for classes early enough to get a schedule that fit around his work hours. Perhaps, though, he really needed to evaluate why he was attending college. A degree was not required for this job he enjoyed and wanted to keep. Waiting to take courses until college was a priority in his life would have helped him have a much better attitude about attending classes.

There might be other activities filling your schedule that need to be examined. Are you making the best use of your time? Do you have enough time reserved for homework and study? Have you set aside time for yourself and for your loved ones? Now look to see where your schedule is blank. These are opportunities for those discretionary activities. A schedule is not meant to be a burden. Instead, think of it as a visual aid to show you when you will be able to do the things you need and want to do. You will also want to make sure that you leave some totally open spaces. Don't schedule every minute of every day. You may need to cope with life's unexpected emergencies.

As you put together your weekly and semester schedules, follow these two rules when planning your college study time:

1. Never schedule yourself to work more than four hours in any one day on the same assignment. Three hours would be better and more reasonable.
2. Always give yourself an extra day.

Most of us want to avoid living in a constant crisis-management mode. Like Sam in our case study, you never know how study plans may go awry. If you wait until the last day to work on a major assignment, an unforeseen emergency could occur that would prevent you from completing your assignment on time. Even minor irritations such as getting sick, having car trouble, getting stuck in traffic for hours, weather complications, etc. can use up those last moments you were counting on to get your work done. If you allow extra time, you won't have to worry. In addition, finishing an assignment early allows you to **proofread** it to make sure it is your best work.

Let's look at a student's semester schedule. Maria has chosen the month-at-a-glance type calendar. From her student handbook, she has identified holidays and other important college dates and transferred them to her calendar. Next, she looked at all of her course syllabi and entered major deadline dates for assignments and tests. Then, she considered her family obligations, social commitments, and known appointments. Finally, she noted her work hours and when she might be able to work overtime to earn extra money. She realized she'd have to plan her study time carefully during the weeks before the holidays.

This semester Maria is taking Introduction to Microsoft Office, English Composition, and a U.S. History telecourse. Since Maria has no computer at home, she needs to spend at least two hours per week in a computer lab. She has an essay due every other Friday in her English class and has specific deadline dates for taking four tests and turning in the research paper in U.S. History. She does have a VCR at home so she will be able to view the history videos at home as well as on campus, and she plans to schedule two viewings per week as often as possible. She wants to finish viewing the history videotapes by Thanksgiving, as her history research paper is due the first week of December. Finishing this class a full week before finals will let her schedule additional time for her computer class if necessary. It will also allow her to work overtime hours to make some extra money for Christmas.

Maria's sister, Carmen, is getting married in November. Maria is going to be in the wedding. She will need to go for a dress fitting and attend a bridal shower, the rehearsal dinner, and the wedding. She comes from a close-knit family; they usually spend holidays together and have regular family gatherings during the semester that she wants to attend.

THIEVES OF TIME

Sometimes even your best efforts at scheduling don't produce the results you want. Have you ever had one of those days where nothing on your to-do list got done? What happened? It's as though a thief broke into your life and stole those minutes and hours that you

September

Sunday	Monday	Tuesday	Wednesday	Thursday	Friday	Saturday
1 Church service	2 **Labor Day** Family picnic noon Work 5–9	3 ENG 8–9:15 CIS 9:35–10:50 CIS Lab 11–12 View history video	4 Work 5–9	5 ENG 8–9:15 CIS 9:35–10:50 CIS Lab 11–12	6 View history video Work 5–9	7 Work 9–5
8 Church service	9 Work 5–9	10 ENG 8–9:15 CIS 9:35–10:50 CIS Lab 11–12	11 View history video Work 5–9	12 ENG 8–9:15 CIS 9:35–10:50 CIS Lab 11–12 ENG essay due	13 Children's program at library 11:00 Work 5–9	14 Work 9–5 Block party
15 Church service Mom's birthday party	16 Work 5–9	17 ENG 8–9:15 **ENG test** CIS 9:35–10:50 CIS Lab 11–12	18 View history video Work 5–9	19 ENG 8–9:15 CIS 9:35–10:50 **(Test)** CIS Lab 11–12	20 View history video Work 5–9	21 Work 9–5
22 Church service	23 **History test** Work 5–9	24 ENG 8–9:15 CIS 9:35–10:50 CIS Lab 11–12	25 View history video Work 5–9	26 ENG 8–9:15 CIS 9:35–10:50 CIS Lab 11–12 ENG essay due	27 View history video **Dental appt.** **11:00 a.m.** Work 5–9	28 Work 9–5 Church service
29 Walkathon	30 **Precollege Pageant** **10:00** Work 5–9					

October

Sunday	Monday	Tuesday	Wednesday	Thursday	Friday	Saturday
		1 ENG 8–9:15 CIS 9:35–10:50 CIS Lab 11–12	2 View history video Work 5–9	3 ENG 8–9:15 CIS 9:35–10:50 CIS Lab 11–12	4 View history video Work 5–9	5 Work 9–5
6 Church service	7 View history video Work 5–9	8 ENG 8–9:15 CIS 9:35–10:50 CIS Lab 11–12	9 **History test** Work 5–9	10 ENG 8–9:15 CIS 9:35–10:50 CIS Lab 11–12 ENG essay due	11 Dress fitting 2:00 Work 5–9	12 Work 9–5
13 Church service View history video	14 Work 5–9	15 ENG 8–9:15 **ENG test** CIS 9:35–10:50 CIS Lab 11–12	16 View history video Work 5–9	17 ENG 8–9:15 CIS 9:35–10:50 CIS Lab 11–12	18 View history video Work 5–9	19 Work 9–5
20 Church service Family dinner	21 Work 5–9	22 ENG 8–9:15 CIS 9:35–10:50 CIS Lab 11–12	23 View history video Work 5–9	24 ENG 8–9:15 CIS 9:35–10:50 CIS Lab 11–12 ENG essay due	25 Dog to Vet 11:00 Work 5–9	26 Work 9–5 Get kids costumes ready
27 Church service 12:30 Bridal Shower	28 View history video **Final dress fitting** **3:00** Work 5–9	29 ENG 8–9:15 CIS 9:35–10:50 CIS Lab 11–12	30 **History test** Work 5–9	31 **Halloween** ENG 8–9:15 CIS 9:35–10:50 CIS Lab 11–12 Trick-or-treat 3:30– 6:00		

November

Sunday	Monday	Tuesday	Wednesday	Thursday	Friday	Saturday
					1 View history video Work 5–9	2 Work 9–5
3 Church service Pancake Breakfast	4 View history video Work 5–9	5 ENG 8–9:15 CIS 9:35–10:50 CIS Lab 11–12	6 **Register for Spring classes** Work 5–9	7 ENG 8–9:15 CIS 9:35–10:50 CIS Lab 11–12 ENG essay due	8 **Rehearsal & Dinner**	9 **Carmen & Mike's Wedding**
10 Church service View history video	11 Holiday Work 5–9 (Overtime pay!)	12 ENG 8–9:15 CIS 9:35–10:50 CIS Lab 11–12	13 View history video Work 5–9	14 ENG 8–9:15 CIS 9:35–10:50 CIS Lab 11–12	15 View history video Work 5–9	16 Work 9–5
17 Church service	18 **History test** Work 5–9	19 ENG 8–9:15 CIS 9:35–10:50 CIS Lab 11–12 **Research Paper Draft Due**	20 **Last date to drop classes** Work 5–9	21 ENG 8–9:15 CIS 9:35–10:50 CIS Lab 11–12 ENG essay due	22 **Dr.'s Appt. at 10:00** Work 5–9	23 Work 9–5
24 Church service	25 Work 5–9	26 ENG 8–9:15 CIS 9:35–10:50 CIS Lab 11–12	27 Work 5–9	28 **Thanksgiving** Work 9–5 (Overtime) Dinner at Mom's 6:00	29 **Break** Work 1–9 (Overtime)	30 Work 9–5

December

Sunday	Monday	Tuesday	Wednesday	Thursday	Friday	Saturday
1 Church service	2 Work 2–9 (Overtime)	3 ENG 8–9:15 CIS 9:35–10:50 CIS Lab 11–12 **Research Paper Due**	4 Work 2–9 (Overtime)	5 ENG 8–9:15 CIS 9:35–10:50 CIS Lab 11–12	6 Work 2–9 (Overtime)	7 Work 9–5
8 Church service Kids rehearsal for Christmas Program 2:00	9 Work 3–9 (Overtime)	10 ENG 8–9:15 CIS 9:35–10:50 CIS Lab 11–12	11 Work 3–9 (Overtime)	12 ENG 8–9:15 CIS 9:35–10:50 CIS Lab 11–12	13 Work 3–9 (Overtime)	14 Work 9–5
15 **Christmas Program** 6:00	16 ← Work 5–9	17 *F I N A L*	18 *E X A M* Work 5–9	19 *W E E K*	20 → Work 1–9	21 Work 9–5 Church service
22 Work Overtime	23 Work Overtime	24 Work Overtime Christmas Eve service	25 **Christmas** Dinner at Mom's 6:00	26 Work Overtime	27 Work Overtime	28 Work 9–5
29 Church service Dinner at Aunt Rosa's	30 Work Overtime	31 **New Year's Eve**				

planned to use for homework and study. Do you remember our friend Sam from the case study?

Several things derailed Sam's study plan. First, he procrastinated writing his English paper until the weekend before it was due. Secondly, he planned to do all of his homework in one afternoon, which really wasn't enough time. Next, he forgot several errands that he then added to his schedule at the last minute. He didn't anticipate getting sidetracked or having to wait in line. He didn't bring work with him to do while he was waiting, so he wasted that time. At home he had several other distractions that interrupted his concentration.

What are some of the common thieves of time that thwart your plans and use up your time?

Procrastination

This is probably the number one time thief. Although it manifests itself in many ways, procrastination comes in two common varieties: *inertia* and *avoidance*. *Inertia* is a word you might remember from science class. It is the physics property that says unless acted upon by a greater force, things in motion stay in motion, and things at rest (motionless) stay at rest. If you've ever had to push a stalled car, you know that it takes more effort to get it going when it's stopped. Once it starts to roll, it takes less effort to keep it going.

How does this relate to you and your use of time? If your body is at rest (such as on the couch watching TV), it will stay at rest unless you force it into action. Sometimes stopping to watch your favorite half-hour show turns into several hours in front of the TV. Once you stop working, it takes more effort to get back to work. That's why many students prefer to schedule breaks between classes so they can study in the library or Learning Resource Center, rather than wait until they get home. If you tend to put things off because it is easier to be lazy, you need to look at your goals and remember your priorities. Tell yourself, "I need to be doing _____ right now."

Overcoming Procrastination

1. Find the first step for whatever it is you have to do. Start there without contemplating the whole project yet. Just get the momentum going.

2. Set a short time limit. Commit to working on your task for 10 or 15 minutes. Sometimes you'll get involved and work longer.

3. Try to understand why you are avoiding a task. Learn to compensate for whatever the reason. If you do not understand, ask the instructor to explain. Perhaps your fellow classmates might be able to help out. Ask them what they know or understand about a given assignment. Seek out tutoring if you need it.

4. Get a study circle going for a particular class or find a study partner. When you make a commitment with others to spend time on a particular class or assignment, it will be easier to stick with a schedule.

Avoidance is the other reason people tend to put off getting things done. They really don't want to do it at all. Have you ever avoided doing something because:

- The task is too hard or too overwhelming?
- If you can't do it perfectly, you don't want to do it at all?

- You don't see any real value in doing it?
- You would rather be doing something else?
- You dislike the task or find it unpleasant?
- You don't want to/are afraid to deal with the problem/situation?
- A distorted self-concept, conscious or unconscious, makes you feel inadequate?
- You are afraid of someone else's judgment of your work?

Distractions

Even the most dedicated student can be thrown off course by distractions. These also come in two varieties: *external* and *internal*. *External distractions* such as noise, music, TV, or computer games come from our surroundings or from other people. Physical problems or limitations such as a room temperature that is too hot or too cold, uncomfortable furniture, or poor lighting may take your mind off the task at hand. Interruptions (whether in person or on the telephone) by family members, friends, salespeople, etc. are some of the most common and irritating external distractions.

Internal distractions come from within and interfere with your ability to concentrate. They could be emotional or relationship problems that upset you and cause you stress; physical needs such as hunger, thirst, fatigue, or illness; negative attitudes about your assignment, instructor, or the course; daydreaming; thinking about other things; worrying; or whatever keeps you from focusing your attention on your studies.

Overcoming Distractions

1. Be aware of your internal and external distracters.
2. When you think of something you need to do or remember, jot it down on a separate sheet of paper and then forget it until after completing your study session.
3. Learn to say "NO" to interruptions; close the door, don't answer the phone, turn off the TV . . .
4. Choose a study location that is as free from external distractions as possible.

Overscheduling

This is a common time thief for many adult students. Because there are so many conflicting demands for our time and energy, we often get overwhelmed with things that appear on our to-do list as either "urgent" or "responsibilities." Trying to do too much at once to meet real or imagined obligations can cause burnout and stress. The inability to say "no" to things/activities may cause us to spend time meeting other people's expectations and not meeting our own. When we get overwhelmed or overly fatigued, our bodies often succumb to a cold or the flu, and we end up "losing" time being sick.

Set daily goals, objectives, and priorities. If you do not have priorities, you could be spending too much time on minor things. We often try to do too much only to find that we are unable to thoroughly complete certain tasks. Recognize that some things may need to be left undone while others may be delegated to someone else. Get your family members to act as a team and help each other out. When one person has a super busy week, someone else could "cover" for him/her with the agreement that the favor will be reciprocated. It could not only reduce your workload, but may even lead to a more harmonious life at home.

Overcoming Overscheduling

1. Be aware of your established college/work/family commitments and limit taking on new responsibilities.

2. Be sure your schedule includes enough sleep time. Studying all night is not as productive as you might think. Research has found that students who got a full night's sleep after studying remembered information twice as well as students who pulled an "all-nighter."

3. Learn to say "no" to people and activities that are not a high priority for you.

Poor Time Management/Organizational Skills

This time thief is subtle. You may not even realize all of the time it consumes. However, if you've ever spent an hour searching for something you "lost" because it wasn't put away properly, you may start to get the idea. Being disorganized with your schoolwork could be hazardous to your grade. For example, your returned quizzes and homework papers can be great study aids for your final exams, but if you aren't able to find them, you can't use them. Your notes and all related papers for each class should be kept together in a notebook. Have a filing system to organize returned, graded papers and keep them until *after you receive your final grade* for the course. If there is a grade dispute, the burden of proof will be up to you.

For many students, the inability to set priorities, confusion about or lack of goals/direction, and poor planning cost a lot of time and money. Sometimes students wait to do academic planning with a counselor or advisor until after they have already spent two or more semesters in college. They are frustrated and angry when they discover that they have taken courses that do not count toward their chosen degree. For students receiving financial aid, the consequences may be especially daunting because the Pell grant will only pay for 150% of the credit hours required for a specific associate degree. (That's 96 hours of coursework toward a typical 64-credit hour degree.) Courses that you fail or from which you withdraw after the refund date count toward the 96-hour total. If you have to take several developmental English and math courses as prerequisites for the ones that satisfy your degree requirements, you need to choose your other courses wisely so you will not exceed the number of courses for which you can receive aid.

There are many old maxims such as "an ounce of prevention is worth a pound of cure," or "a stitch in time saves nine" that attempt to teach us some truths about time management. Putting things off and not taking time to plan or prepare properly have proven to be much more time consuming in the long run.

Overcoming Poor Organization

1. Have all of your supplies and study materials ready so you won't waste time or get distracted looking for them.

2. Have a notebook and filing system for each course. Keep everything for that course together. Organize your notebook with tab dividers so you can quickly find what you need.

3. Break tasks into smaller chunks. Set a pace, give yourself deadlines, and reward yourself for what you have accomplished. When you become bored with what you are studying, change the task.

4. Write a to-do list. As you cross off those items you complete, you will feel a sense of accomplishment. It will allow you to see and chart your progress and will provide self-satisfaction that might become one of your best motivators.

5. Plan a ten-minute break after each study hour. If you tend to abuse your breaks, set a timer to get back on task.

TIPS FOR MAXIMIZING YOUR TIME

You can't really "save" time, but you can learn to spend less time on unimportant tasks, leaving you more time for the things that matter most. Here are a few tips that we've read or learned through experience. See if any of them fit your needs:

- Put everything in the proper place immediately so you will not have to retrace your steps.
- Handle mail and other such paper only once. Open your mail by the wastebasket or recycling bin. Decide immediately what to discard, and do it.
- **Always** have something to do (from your list) in case you have to wait. Review with your flash cards, read a few pages of a book, balance your checkbook, go over your to-do lists, etc., and take advantage of time that would otherwise be wasted.
- Combine chores and trips. On your way to the store, stop at the gas station, the bank, and the cleaners.
- Determine your best time of day to study. Use it whenever possible.
- When you begin your studies, concentrate on one thing at a time.
- Plan in the morning and set priorities for the day. If you are more of an evening person, do your planning at night for the next day.
- Make a list of everything you have to do to complete a specific project and set a target date for completion of each step. For an English paper, you might set dates for choosing a topic, completing the research, writing an outline, finishing a first draft, typing the paper, and editing and/or proofreading the paper.
- Don't be afraid to ask for help when you need it.
- Ask yourself, "What is the best possible use of my time *right now*?"

SUMMARY

Most students have multiple roles (student, employee, family member, etc.) and have many demands on their time. Unfortunately, study time is often sacrificed to do other things. Careful use of your time is critical to success in college. Learning to set specific, realistic, and measurable goals is the first step toward developing a workable time management plan. Identify your long- and short-term goals, and give priority to the activities that assist you in achieving them.

This chapter introduced three scheduling tools, **the weekly schedule, the semester schedule,** and **the daily to-do list,** that can help you keep track of how you need/wish to spend your time. It also discussed some of the common "thieves of time," such as **procrastination, distraction, over-commitment, and poor planning.**

JOURNAL QUESTIONS

Write a one-page (or longer) typed essay to respond to the following:

1. What are the biggest time management problems experienced by Sam or Maria?
   What recommendations would you make that would be most helpful to them? Why?

2. What time management issues have you identified in your own life? What solutions can you
   generate?

EXERCISE 1.

Using your current schedule and your semester calendar, make up a weekly schedule for next week using the chart on the following page. Be sure to indicate your class times, work hours, and study times along with your regular activities. Be as detailed as possible. You may draw arrows to indicate activities that last longer than an hour or occur every day at the same time. Most time periods should be filled.

	SUNDAY	MONDAY	TUESDAY	WEDNESDAY	THURSDAY	FRIDAY	SATURDAY
4:00–5:00 a.m.							
5:00–6:00 a.m.							
6:00–7:00 a.m.							
7:00–8:00 a.m.							
8:00–9:00 a.m.			computer class ↓	computer class ↓			
9:00–10:00 a.m.							
10:00–11:00 a.m.			graphic class ↓	graphic class ↓			
11:00–12:00 p.m.							
12:00–1:00 p.m.							
1:00–2:00 p.m.							
2:00–3:00 p.m.		drawing class ↓	math class ↓	drawing class ↓			
3:00–4:00 p.m.							
4:00–5:00 p.m.							
5:00–6:00 p.m.							
6:00–7:00 p.m.							
7:00–8:00 p.m.							
8:00–9:00 p.m.							
9:00–10:00 p.m.							
10:00–11:00 p.m.							
11:00–12:00 p.m.							
12:00–1:00 a.m.							
1:00–2:00 a.m.							
2:00–3:00 a.m.							
3:00–4:00 a.m.							

Chapter 3

Learning Strategies for Academic Success

*I am convinced that it is of primordial importance to learn more every year
than the year before. After all, what is education but a process by which a person
begins to learn how to learn?"*

—PETER USTINOV

This chapter provides specific strategies to help students learn information at the level required by most college courses. It begins with information about your brain and how you receive and process information. Next, **Bloom's Taxonomy** of Educational Objectives is introduced. This classification system explains levels of thinking and how this relates to learning strategies. The chapter offers specific study strategies and techniques for an effective study session, time management, listening, note-taking, memory, concentration, writing, test taking, and textbook reading. Every semester will be a continual process of learning about yourself as a learner. Each course will require that you try different learning strategies that match the level of knowledge required by the course.

UNDERSTANDING HOW YOU LEARN

Frequently, first-year students enter college classrooms experiencing feelings of apprehension and curiosity. Relatives, friends, and high school teachers may have told you college courses will be vastly different and much harder than high school classes. What is different? What makes college classes so difficult? Why are some classes easier than you expected? What strategies can you learn to cope with new academic challenges? Are you academically ready? Thinking about all these questions can be challenging, confusing, and perplexing.

When you are overwhelmed, the best idea is to take a deep breath and start at the beginning. The first step for assessing your academic readiness is to set aside some time and analyze your **PBID**. What is PBID? Before you begin a new physical activity, such as snowboarding, skiing, or skateboarding, you check your physical readiness. Well, now you need to check four factors, **Purpose, Background, Interest, and Difficulty (PBID)**, that affect your academic readiness; that is, your ability to be successful learning new course information.

Purpose is the reason why you enroll in a course. Why does it matter what your reason is for enrolling in a class? Humans tend to match their behavior to their purpose or goals. Purposes that are unclear (or are based on someone else's goal) may hamper your desire to succeed in the course.

Background knowledge gives you the ability to link new information to previously learned concepts. The more background you have in a subject, the easier it is to make more connections and apply information beyond rote learning. Also, high background knowledge in a subject motivates you to learn more, so your learning can become more purposeful.

Interest is the factor that captures your attention. Think of how easily your attention can be caught by the tabloids at the checkout stand! Your lack of interest could be related to a fuzzy purpose for taking the course or even lack of background knowledge in the course. It is difficult to be interested in something you don't know anything about. If your attention is not captured, then you will have to create strategies that involve you in the material.

Difficulty can be a combination of many factors. It could be related to the course content, lack of background, lack of motivation, or the manner in which the course is taught.

Use Figure 1 to assess your PBID. Knowing your PBID and learning about how your brain processes information will help you create the learning strategies you need to be successful.

Learning how individuals receive, store, and retrieve information from the brain is important. This information will help you create strategies to learn material in the most effective manner and then store the facts for future use. Because people make sense of the world based on what they already know, information is learned by connecting new information with the knowledge already in place. How the information travels to the brain, connects with previous information, and then is converted to memory is unique for each individual. This is their **learning style**. Most of us prefer learning in the style or format that is easiest for us to comprehend, to store, and retrieve.

Three main sensory paths carry information to the brain: visual, auditory, and kinesthetic. **Visual learners** learn best through visual processing; that is, using their eyes to learn information. To remember information, they need to see it presented visually, as in a chart or diagram or written down. Reading textbooks and obtaining new information in a visual format is the easiest method of learning for these students. They enjoy lecture classes and take many notes to study after class. They often are most comfortable with instructors who use the blackboard to illustrate important concepts or distribute lecture notes or outlines of the lecture.

Auditory learners process information best through their auditory system. They prefer to learn by hearing the information, as in listening to lectures. The auditory learner likes discussion and usually learns well in a study group or with a study partner. Auditory learners often need to hear what a difficult passage sounds like or to talk out a difficult concept before they read the textbook. Their recall is increased when they practice teaching the concept to someone else.

Kinesthetic learners like to associate movement with their learning. They prefer the sense of touch and actually learn better when they are physically involved in what they are studying. They are good at applied, hands-on tasks. They usually find *doing* to be the best way of learning. Strategies that incorporate movement are the most effective for them. Activities

Assessing Your PBID For Learning Readiness

Purpose: Why are you taking this class?

◆ It is required for my major, for general education.

◆ I need the information to build my background for another subject.

◆ I hope there is information and/or skills I can use to develop my learning skills.

◆ My best friend told me it would be easy.

◆ It was all I could find to fit my schedule.

Background: What do I already know about this subject?

◆ I have had previous classes in this subject.

◆ I have had personal experience with this subject.

◆ I have limited knowledge of the subject.

Interest: Do I like studying this subject?

◆ Other students told me about the class, and I have some questions I hope will be answered by the class.

◆ I really have little interest in this class, but my advisor told me I had to take it.

◆ I am looking at a major related to this subject.

◆ This class will provide information about a hobby that I have.

Difficulty: How difficult do you expect material in the class to be, and how much time do you anticipate you'll have to spend on the class?

◆ I expect the class will be really easy, and I won't have to study much for it.

◆ Studying has always been hard for me, and I don't expect it to be any different in this class.

◆ This particular subject has <u>always</u> been challenging for me.

◆ I have heard this was a very tough class with a difficult instructor.

Figure 1 Assessing your PBID

such as walking through a demonstration or project, writing down information, and applying it to real-life circumstances are helpful. Movements, such as tapping on the desk, jiggling their legs up and down, and clicking their pens as they study, actually enable them to concentrate and learn. They are most comfortable getting up and walking around while studying, writing lists, outlining chapters, using note cards, and manipulating and moving information around. Strategies that involve music and rhythm, or acting or role playing, may be helpful. (Remember the songs that helped you learn all the names of the fifty states or even the alphabet?)

The sensory path which you tend to use most frequently characterizes your learning style. Most learners make use of all three sensory paths, but many students find themselves relying heavily on one and not always their strongest one. Think of how someone has tried to teach you a skill, such as a new computer program, and you became frustrated that you didn't catch on quickly. Perhaps the instructor explained the process to you, but you needed to read the directions for yourself. When you read the information and then listened to the instructor, you caught on quickly. The strongest learning link occurs when you combine two or more learning styles. It is important to remember that combining your preferred learning style with a different learning style may enhance your learning and increase your retention. This ability to adapt your style will be important as you meet instructors with many teaching styles who use a variety of techniques. The Sensory Modality Exercise at the end of the chapter will help you begin to discover what type of learner you are. The chart in **Figure 2** outlines strategies for studying based on your learning style preference.

Visual Learners	**Auditory Learners**	**Kinesthetic Learners**
Mark important information using a color system.	Lecture to yourself.	Study with another person.
Draw charts, graphs, or diagrams.	Work in study groups.	Have a dialogue with yourself about the material.
Form pictures to which you can attach the information being learned.	Discuss or teach others the material.	Use note cards to record and organize necessary information.
Copy or type notes into an outline format.	Read notes or material aloud.	Match the information to movement (tap a pencil, swing your foot).
	Read notes into a tape recorder, then listen.	Stand up; walk around.
		Demonstrate your knowledge to others.
		Use a hands-on-approach.

Figure 2   Learning Style Study Strategies

LEVELS OF THINKING

A major distinction between the high school and college class environment is that college faculty expect students to assume responsibility for their own learning of information. Instructors do not check to see if students have purchased textbooks, if they are taking notes, keeping up with the reading assignments, or studying for tests. Attending classes is the responsibility of the student, and many instructors do not penalize students for absences. At first, students may not perceive that the classes are difficult, but this perception often changes after the first exam. College classes often require a level of learning that students may not have incorporated into their previous learning strategies. Most high school courses focus on lower levels of understanding. Often students only needed to recognize the correct answer or restate information. Postsecondary coursework assumes students already know how to do that. They require you to think differently and at higher levels.

Many students find that the self-taught study strategies that enabled them to be successful in high school do not transfer to the college environment. Your high school or job-related experiences developed skills that you can now build upon and expand. Also, your previous study skills can be used as a base to learn more strategies. When you learn more about effective learning and study skills, then you can design your learning time to produce results. *You will not have to work harder, but you will be working smarter.*

Bloom's Taxonomy. Luckily, you already know how to think and are aware that different tasks require different degrees of thinking. The thinking you do when you remember a phone number differs from the thinking you do to solve a math story problem. If you can identify the level of thinking you already do, the level you may need to achieve, then you can apply this knowledge to areas involved in studying coursework. Figure 3 shows the levels of thinking according to a system called Bloom's Taxonomy. Each level builds on the previous level. That is, students cannot speak and comprehend a foreign language until they have

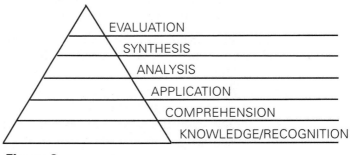

Figure 3

memorized the basic vocabulary. Effective students are aware of learning strategies that incorporate the level of thinking required for success in each course.

Knowledge and **recognition** of information are the first level and form the basis of understanding. It requires you to remember what you heard or read, but not necessarily to understand it. It is as simple as remembering the name of the person you just met or what you need at the grocery store. In coursework, this level is necessary to build information for any subject. Many general education courses you select will require you to learn the basic vocabulary and principles of the course. Memorization can achieve this, but this is not meaningful learning, which requires understanding of the material.

The comprehension level emphasizes studying for an understanding of the material you are trying to learn. In this level of Bloom's taxonomy, you become more focused on what the material is trying to explain to you. At this level, you can explain information to someone else. You can share the plot of a movie or a novel, report the homework assignment to a roommate who missed class, or explain the course syllabus.

The third level in Bloom's taxonomy is **application**. When you apply what you understand, you begin to link the information you gained to examples in your own life. After seeing a movie or reading a novel, you connect with similar personal experiences. Your ability to see a parallel between an example in a text and the experience in your own life is the thinking skill of application. At this level, math courses require students to solve word problems or solve problems different from those previously seen. You are asked to compare and contrast information on an essay test question. Many courses will ask you to provide examples from your own life of the information you study, determine causes and effects, or draw analogies. The more ways you apply the information, the longer you will retain the concepts.

Analysis requires you to break apart and examine the components of a concept in depth. Depth is the key element that true analysis demands. If when discussing a movie or novel with a friend, you discuss the main theme and what made the leading character so evil, then you are using analytical thinking skills. If your friend disagrees with your analysis and questions your theory, the friendly debate that may follow requires additional analytic thinking.

Synthesis is the creative level of thinking. You combine different ideas to create a new whole. When you synthesize, you combine your current understanding of concepts with new information that you create. Many instructors assign group projects where students must design, create, or propose a solution to a problem. Examples that require that you operate at a synthesizing level include using music or art to express yourself, developing a topic for a research paper, or answering essay questions that ask you to "tie together" all the information you have learned to solve a problem.

Evaluation forms the highest level of thinking in Bloom's taxonomy. At this level, you must use your personal judgment regarding an issue's relevance, depth, value, or other qualities. To do this, you would review all the relevant "facts" and review sources for their contribution to the topic under discussion. You often use evaluation to make judgments and decisions in your personal life. Choosing to attend college, whether to live on or off campus, or how many hours you can work and still do well in school require evaluation. Coursework may ask you to evaluate decisions in court cases or whether a social policy is adequate in providing aid and assistance to poor people. Geography classes may require you to judge what types of vegetation could adapt to climatic changes.

Although this chapter describes the levels of Bloom's taxonomy separately, few learning situations depend solely on one level or another. Generally, as the information increases in complexity, the effort needed to learn also increases. Your classes will increase in complexity as will the levels of thinking required, as you specialize in a content area. This information will help you as a learner continually decide what you know, what you still need to learn, and the ways in which you must learn. The study strategies noted in Figure 4, along with examples from this chapter, will help you in applying this information as you study.

STUDY SESSION STRATEGIES

How much should I study? As a rule of thumb, you will need to plan to study every day for every class. The recommended time is two hours of study for every hour of class. When you set up your study times, be sure to avoid marathon study sessions. Studying for 40–50 minutes and then taking a ten minute break is much more effective than trying to cram for 2–3 hours without stopping. The reason for this is that you remember best what you studied at the beginning and the end of the study session. We most quickly forget material learned in the middle. Therefore, shorter study sessions, with frequent breaks, are recommended. A word of caution—the break should be a non-TV break and should not last longer than the study session itself!

Where should I study? An important part of being successful at studying is setting up the appropriate environment for studying. Do you have a regular place to study? Is that place free of distractions? Does it contain all of the supplies you will need for studying? Is there proper lighting and ventilation? If most of your responses to these questions are "no," then maybe the first thing you need to do is make some changes in your study environment. The following suggestions will help you.

An effective study environment is:

- *A regular place.* By establishing a regular place, you are forming a habit. The habit is "when I sit at this area, I study and learn information." The more you practice that habit, the easier it will become. Think about your behavior. If you continually jump up to find something to eat, that is the habit you are establishing.

- *Free of distractions.* Unfortunately for most of us, a distraction-free environment is not possible. Distractions come in many forms and differ for individuals. Generally, the two greatest distractors are noise and motion. You will want to try to study in a place that is relatively quiet. This might mean that you need to rethink your choice of locations or possibly change your time for studying. Students with families quite often find it easier to stay at school and study in the library or in another open study area on campus. You will want to explore some options for a study place. The important thing is to find a consistent spot that works for you.

- *Designed to contain all of the supplies you need for studying.* To be most efficient in studying, you should have everything you need in close proximity before beginning. Having your math book in the back of your roommate's car and your roommate on the way to Chicago is not a good way to start a study session. By establishing a regular and consistent place to study, you are also able to make sure that this place contains all the supplies you will be needing: pens, pencils, highlighters, calculators, scrap paper, dictionary, a thesaurus, etc.

- *Properly lit and ventilated.* Lighting is an important part of your learning environment. Students typically spend a great deal of their time reading textbooks. Ideally, your study area should be well lit; otherwise, eye strain from improper lighting may result in decreased concentration. A room that is too hot or too cold will be distracting to you. Rooms that are not properly ventilated tend to get uncomfortable. You may find yourself falling asleep or unable to concentrate if the room is too warm or improperly ventilated. A cold room can make you tense and reduce your ability to concentrate.

- *Not too comfortable.* Many students try to study in bed and then can't figure out why they are always falling asleep. A bed is for sleeping! That is a habit that is well established. If you choose a place that is too comfortable, you will find that you are often unable to stay awake. Students, as a rule, tend to burn the candle at both ends, working, studying, playing, etc. Sleep deprivation appears to be common among students. It is natural that when you finally settle into a comfortable place you begin to nod off.

Definition and Examples for the Six Thinking/Learning Levels

1. **Knowledge/Recall/Recognition.** Remembering factual information.

   Define, identify, label, state, list, match, write
   ▼ What is evapotranspiration?
   ▼ Identify the standard peripheral components of a computer.
   ▼ Write the equation for the Ideal Gas Law.

2. **Comprehension.** Understanding, summarizing, and explaining the meaning of information.

   Describe, restate, generalize, paraphrase, summarize, estimate
   ▼ Describe the different climates and the characteristics of each.
   ▼ Give an example of positive reinforcement.
   ▼ State in your own words the meaning of functionalism.

3. **Application.** Using abstractions in concrete or practical situations.

   Determine, chart, implement, prepare, solve, use, develop
   ▼ Using the Koppen System, describe the importance of another classification system for climate.
   ▼ What type of reinforcement is being used when one roommate cleans up after another?
   ▼ If a person has psychogenic shock, what should you do for them?

4. **Analysis.** Breaking down a whole into component parts.

   Point out, differentiate, distinguish, discriminate, compare, explain
   ▼ Compare and contrast the major assumptions underlying psychoanalytic and humanistic approaches to psychology.
   ▼ Explain the patriarchal society in terms of lineage and dominance of the sexes.

5. **Synthesis.** Putting parts together to form a new and integrated whole; combining facts into new ideas.

   Create, design, plan, organize, generate, develop
   ▼ Develop and write a logically organized essay in favor of euthanasia.
   ▼ Design an individualized nutrition program for a diabetic patient.

6. **Evaluation.** Making judgments about the merits of ideas, theories, or phenomena.

   Appraise, critique, judge, weigh, evaluate, select
   ▼ Assess the appropriateness of the author's conclusions based on the evidence given.
   ▼ Select the best proposal for a proposed water treatment plant.
   ▼ Evaluate a work of art using appropriate terminology.

Figure 4

What should I study? The first step in beginning to study is knowing what to study. Your guideline for knowing what to study will be the class syllabus. The syllabus is an informal contract between you and your professor. The syllabus will usually include a list of course topics, assigned readings, dates of quizzes, exams, and other required assignments. In addition, the syllabus usually provides the instructor's expectations for class participation, attendance, and the grading criteria. You will want to read your syllabus very carefully and make note of all the requirements.

How should I study? Once you know what the course requires, you will need to decide how you are going to study. Your syllabus will be your guide to creating specific study goals. You create study goals by thinking of the product you want at the end of the study session. In addition, the level of knowledge required by the information should guide your studying. Are you aiming for a strict knowledge level where memorization of terms will suffice? What is the testing format of the course? Will there be essay questions on the exam? Does this mean you should comprehend and explain your answers? Setting specific study goals can be difficult. It will take practice for you to be able to distinguish a specific goal from a nonspecific goal. Too often students confuse a broad, general declaration of intent to study with a specific, measurable study goal. The following are examples of specific study goals, based on a desired product.

- I will complete a written outline or summary of the main points in chapter one.
- I will formulate three questions for each major heading in chapter one.
- I will answer the questions at the end of the chapter.
- I will define all of the terms listed in the chapter summary.

By formulating specific, measurable study goals at the beginning of your study session, you then have a way of knowing when you are finished studying, and you have a concrete product. You can create a study guide—a chapter summary, possible test questions, solved problems, or a list of defined terms. These products can be utilized as review tools for future study sessions.

Group and individual studying. Often there are classes with large amounts of information, and knowing what to study or even where to begin can be challenging. If your instructor expects you to comprehend and apply the information, it is wise to practice doing this before an exam. Many students find that studying in a group is a more effective way to organize and learn information. Students benefit from considering information from another point of view or learning style perspective.

TIME MANAGEMENT STRATEGIES

Effective time management will be your most important study strategy. To new college students facing academic, social, and personal demands, there never seems to be enough time. The academic environment presents new opportunities and challenges that appear to demand more time than you may think you have. You can't create more time, but you can become more skilled at how you manage time. Time management involves setting goals, planning, flexibility, commitment, and managing procrastination.

Goal setting. Managing time and setting goals go hand-in-hand. Using your time wisely helps you to achieve what you want, when you want. Knowing what your goals are for college and your future career help guide decisions regarding the use of your time.

There are several types of goals:

- *Short-range or immediate*: Goals you want to achieve tomorrow, next week, or within the semester. (Attend class each week, find a study partner for each class, or locate the free math tutor services.)
- *Mid-range*: Goals you want to achieve within 2–3 years. (Complete all the general education requirements.)
- *Long-range*: Goals you want to achieve within 5 years. (Obtain a degree in biology.)

Establishing goals can be difficult. The following guidelines will help you:

- Goals must be related to your **values**. You will find it very difficult to pursue a goal that is not directly linked to something that is important and meaningful for you. For example, if the goal is to pursue a career in social work, but you do not value interpersonal relationships, it will be difficult to succeed in accomplishing it.
- Goals are **specific and concrete**. A goal must state exactly what you are going to do. It can't be some vague, hopeful wish. A goal to stop procrastinating sounds nice, but it is not specific. A specific goal would state, "I will write a study plan by the end of the first week of class so that I can finish my paper in English by the tenth week of the semester."
- Goals are **measurable**. Progress toward completion of the goal needs to be evaluated. ("I must select my paper topic by the fourth week of class to finish my paper by midterm. When my paper is typed and bound by the day before it is due, I will have completed my goal.")
- Goals are **realistic**. Your goal must be attainable, taking into consideration personal resources and abilities. (If you have not taken an algebra class in high school, it is not realistic to register for calculus, before taking algebra.)
- Goals are **time framed**. Always set a beginning and end date for your goal.
- Goals are **written**. Committing a goal to writing makes it more concrete. It encourages you to be committed to completing it. A goal written on a piece of paper tacked to your bulletin board or written in your daily planner is difficult to ignore.
- Goals are **shared**. Telling someone else of your goals establishes accountability. You will be less likely to procrastinate or waver in your commitment to attaining the goal. Be sure to tell someone who will support you in your efforts to complete your goal.
- Goals need to be **flexible**. There are many factors that can affect attaining a goal. Rarely is a goal followed through to completion without any problems. Temporary setbacks that will interrupt progress are common. These interruptions do not have to keep you from reaching the goal. Instead, reexamine your plan, revise or make a new one. You may discover that the original time frame is unrealistic. Changing the goal may be necessary (you may have reassessed what is important to you). This is okay, as long as the revisions are a way to ensure success versus avoiding doing something you really don't want to do.

Planning. Your goals indicate where you want to go. Creating an action plan tells you how to get there. The saying, "if you don't know where you are going, you may end up somewhere else," is a good reminder of what happens without planning. The plan may consist of your "to do lists," as well as your daily and semester planning schedules. Using these planning tools, write down specifically what you will do, and when and where you will do it. It is through a plan that "time management" becomes tangible and visible. It is no longer a "wish" or a "hope." Plans put you in charge of your time.

Flexibility and commitment. Students need to allow for changes in schedules and plans. There are students who feel that writing their schedules is too rigid; that a written plan does not allow them to relax and enjoy life. But, in order to achieve a goal, there must be a basic commitment to accomplish what you set out to do. Yes, there should be flexibility and time to relax, but with the dedication to return to the plan. Often students use procrastination as an example of incorporating flexibility into their planning. You need to be honest with yourself and ask if procrastinating will detract from your commitment to accomplishing your goal. For many, procrastination is a barrier to accomplishing their goals. It is important to identify the reasons for procrastination, and then take action to overcome the barrier.

Reasons for procrastination. Students' causes for procrastination tend to fit under the following categories:

- *Unrealistic expectations.* Expectations placed upon you by yourself, family, and friends can often result in an overcrowded schedule. You may be able to overdo it for a semester, but over the long haul, it is necessary to realistically define expectations in accordance to personal resources of time, talent, and energy.

- *Erroneous beliefs about academic work.* Many students believe that it is easy to learn and that smart people don't have to study. This belief leads to the further belief that studying is "unnatural." The truth is that learning anything new takes time and effort. People who appear to know everything without studying have usually spent time and effort in the past learning the information.

- *Fear of failure.* For some students, the fear of failing is so great that they avoid ever starting a project. Or there is the fear that they are doing the task "wrong." To manage this fear, you will have to face it and separate information about your performance from your feelings or ideas about your own self-worth. In addition, you may need to ask questions and get more information about the task, so that you can begin with more confidence. Information tells you how to improve; it doesn't say anything about whether you're an OK person.

- *Loss of control.* In the academic world, it is easy to lose control. Other people appear to always be telling you what you must and can do. In many instances, you will have no choices. In response to this lack of control, many students give up or postpone accomplishing required tasks. By identifying what areas of your life you can control, and accepting the others as part of life, you will be better able to handle this feeling of being out of control.

Managing procrastination. You can manage, and in some instances, overcome the procrastination habit. The following strategies may work for you:

- *Pay attention to your excuses (red flags).* "Just this one TV show, and then I'll study." "I work best under pressure." "It's already too late." When you hear yourself saying these things, you know you need to get to work, even if for only five minutes.
- *Optimize your chance for success.* Develop a study routine, including a specific place to study that is conducive to good "brain work." Identify specific goals you want to accomplish during your study session. ("I will read three chapters in Biology." "I will review last week's notes in Math,"etc.)
- *Find people who will be supportive.* Find study partners, study groups, or friends who can motivate you to study when you don't feel like it.
- *Work during your "prime" times.* We all have certain times of the day when we are more energetic and intellectually alert. Do your most difficult work during these hours.
- *Use the "divide and conquer" method.* This involves taking an overwhelming project, like writing a 30-page research paper, and breaking it down into small tasks. Go to the library for 30 minutes to get topic ideas; take an hour to search the library database to narrow the topic; take two hours to develop an outline, etc. Breaking a big project into small, manageable tasks creates a sense of accomplishment and control of the task.
- *Don't wait until you feel like it—there is never a "perfect" time.* Tell yourself you will work for just five minutes. Usually, once you start working, it is easier to continue.
- *Reward yourself.* Set up appropriate rewards when you meet your study goals. "If I read all my chapters in English and outline the major points, I will watch my two favorite TV shows."
- *You don't have to be perfect.* The results of your work have nothing to do with who you are as a person. Don't fall into the trap of believing that you need to "do twice as much just to feel half as good."

In summary, how you organize your time will affect your success in the academic environment.

LISTENING STRATEGIES

Hearing is a physiological, involuntary, natural reaction that does not require interpretation. We know the "muzak" was on in the elevator, but we can't name the song we just heard. In contrast, listening is a psychological, voluntary action that requires interpretation or the assignment of meaning. You must be able to respond to information heard in classes. These are critical skills for a student to develop. Ability in this area will affect your ability to take effective notes that will enhance your success in many classes. Effective listening involves paying attention and concentrating on what the speaker is saying. In order to listen effectively, you must be physically present and mentally alert in class.

Physically present. Being physically present means attending class regularly. If you are not attending regularly, you need to honestly evaluate your situation. Circumstances often necessitate a change in plans. If attending class is not a priority, maybe you need to sit down with an advisor and discuss your academic goals.

Physical presence also means sitting in class where you can hear and see the speaker, focusing on the speaker, and maintaining eye contact. Finding a place to sit where you can see and hear enhances your ability to concentrate. As a general rule, the closer to the front you sit, the more focused and attentive to the lecturer you will remain. In fact, research on college students and academic success has proven that students who sit closer to the instructor achieve higher grades. Those students appear to be more focused on the instructor. From the instructor's perspective he/she may feel that a rapport has been established with those students.

Mentally alert. Being mentally alert means avoiding distractions, thoughts, and behaviors that inhibit or block your ability to listen effectively. Bringing your body to class and allowing your mind to be someplace else sabotages your goals for effective listening. If you are preoccupied, worried, daydreaming, or thinking about something else while trying to listen, you will most likely miss a lot of the information being given. Financial concerns, academic difficulties, family problems, roommates, weekend plans, etc., are all examples of things that compete for a student's attention. For some students, class time is the only quiet time they have. It is during this quiet time that personal problems and concerns begin to enter into consciousness and compete for attention. What can you do when you are sitting in class and your mind begins to wander, or you begin to think about things unrelated to the class?

- Jot down these thoughts on a piece of paper. Tell yourself that you will get back to them later.
- Give yourself permission to attend to these problems at a later time.
- Set aside time during the day to work on problems.

Aside from personal distractions, many students have difficulty listening to lectures because they lack the basic course knowledge. They are unfamiliar with the material being presented and become overwhelmed. This is often the result of failing to do assigned readings or poor class attendance. By attending class regularly, doing supplemental readings to build background, and coming prepared, you are able to keep on top of assignments and avoid being overwhelmed.

Ways to improve listening. There are ways to improve your listening skills. The following is a list of some basic techniques for effective listening in class.

- *Recognize how ideas are organized.* Lectures usually begin with some type of introduction followed by a thesis statement. This statement is what the professor hopes to cover in the day's lecture. The thesis is supported by additional information. Most professors bring closure to their lectures by summarizing what they have covered. Learn to identify the lecture style that is used by your professor.
- *Become involved in what is being said.* If there are prepared notes for the course, read these before coming to class. Think about the purpose of the lecture, identify key points, make connections between ideas, and write down specific examples. Mark possible test questions.

- *Screen out distractions such as:*
  · background noise;
  · unusual accents, dialects, and language mistakes;
  · speaker disorganization, emotion, or habits;
  · superfluous material; and
  · your own inner voice.
- *Organize* statements into main points and supporting reasons. Use an outline form if it is helpful. Add information to prepared notes or outlines.
- *Discriminate* between relevancies and irrelevancies. Remember that not all information is important.
- *Maintain* an active body state. Sit with your back fairly straight and your pen poised to take notes. Sit in front and have eye-contact with the speaker.
- *Develop* a positive attitude about the class. You may have to use "self-talk" statements such as, "I'm going to listen carefully for the key points, so I will be ready for the discussion in my study group."

In order to improve your listening skills, you will need to practice using the suggested techniques for effective listening until they become automatic. There are many situations in which you will have this opportunity—in class, at work, and with friends, family, and strangers.

NOTE-TAKING STRATEGIES

It is difficult to separate listening and note-taking. Note-taking actually aids in effective listening. By taking notes, you are forced to listen carefully and critically to what is being said. You can build your interest in a subject through concentrated listening. Note-taking provides a written aid for the retention of information. When you take notes in class, you are actively processing information.

Taking notes in class involves more than showing up to class with a pen and a piece of paper. It is an active process that involves three stages: before the lecture, during the lecture, and after the lecture.

Before the lecture. Being prepared to take effective notes involves thinking about the process before the actual class period.

- For each class, use a different standard-sized notebook (8½" x 11") or use colored dividers to create sections in one notebook. The larger size allows you to take notes and jot down questions and comments.
- Read the syllabus and discover the topic for that day. Write the date and the topic at the top of the paper.
- Create a note-taking format for that particular class. Formats vary and there is no right way, only the way that works best for you and matches the information in the class. Figure 5 is an example of a popular format called the Cornell method. Divide your paper into separate sections. Choose a main section to take notes and smaller

sections for pertinent information, such as key terms, vocabulary, important people, and dates. Include a section for questions and an area to write a short summary in your own words. Additional sections may be added for supplementary information, for example, a comparison with the textbook information or possibly a section on problem solving.

- Be prepared for the class by reading the textbook assignment or reviewing information from the previous class.
- If the instructor has provided prepared notes for the class, read these before coming to class. (See Figure 6.) This will provide you with background knowledge which will increase your understanding of the lecture.

During the lecture. Now that you have prepared yourself for the process, you are ready for the actual recording of the notes.

- Only record the essential points. Instructors usually indicate important material in a variety of ways, such as:
  - Writing important information on the board.
  - Putting important information onto overheads.
  - Emphasizing important information through tone or voice level.
  - Reviewing or summarizing possible exam material.
  - Restating the same material in several ways.
- Listen for "signal words" from the instructor. These words indicate the direction in which the instructor is headed. (See Figure 10.) Your notes should reflect the signals they gave you such as "There are four important parts of this concept." Then your notes should be labeled accordingly.
- Write on every other line allowing room for additional material.
- Skip lines to show the end of one idea and the start of another. Indicate sub-ideas and supporting details with numbers or letters under the major idea.
- Use abbreviations and symbols when possible. You will want to develop your own personalized vocabulary of symbols that you can use without extra thought. Be careful that you don't use so many types that you can't decipher your notes later. Common symbols are "?" placed by confusing information or "*" by important information to remember. Use abbreviated words such as "i.e." for "in other words" or "ex" for example.
- Write legibly. Do your notes right the first time. This will save you time, as well as giving you practice in listening and taking effective notes.
- Purchased notes should also include active processing during the lecture:
  - Add additional examples given by the instructor or classmates.
  - Star important points stressed by the instructor. (Colored pens are a helpful tool.)
  - Mark confusing points with a question mark. Ask instructor or take questions to a study group.
  - Draw lines to connecting information.
  - Additional information to charts, graphs, or diagrams.

Geog	Climatic Classification	September 5
(2 1/2″ margin for questions, key words, terms, important dates, or people.)	(6″ column for taking notes)	
Köppen	_System of Climatic Classification_	
	–Invented by Wladimir Köppen	
Why is he important?	_–A botanist who saw biological activities as a function of_	
	Climatic characteristics.	
Climograph	_Created a climograph_	
	–Displays monthly temperature and precipitation on one graph	
How do you calculate	_Making it simple: Main Concern_	
problem on a climograph?	_–the relationship between potential evap. & amount of_	
	mois. received at any geog. location.	
What are the characteristics of	_Arctic Climates – Symbols ET and EF_	
E Climates?	_–E climates have aver. monthly temp. <50_	
	ET – Tundra or Continental Subartic	
	Aver temp in warmest month 50 F and <32 F	
	ET – Ice Cap or Arctic	
	Aver. temp in warmest month <32 F	
Boundary calculations?	_The Humid dry boundary_	
	Marks the major difference between a humid and a dry	
	Climate regime	
	Must know how boundary is calculated	
	(2″ space for a possible summary, creating test questions,	
	cross reference with other notes or material.)	
	What is the key importance of temperature and precipitation?	

Figure 5 Sample Notes Using the Cornell Format

After the lecture. Even though class time is over, the note-taking process continues until you have processed your notes for future study.

- Review your notes as soon as possible. Read through them, making corrections and filling in information you remember.
- Depending on your note-taking format, list the key concept words, or main dates, people, etc. in a separate column. In the place you left for a summary, write a summary paragraph and possible test questions.
- Review your notes several times per week, each time adding more information that you remember, or creating more possible test questions.
- Use different-colored highlighters or pens to mark key terms, definitions, dates, important people, examples, etc.

If you are having trouble taking notes in a particular class, make an appointment to meet with your instructor, and let him/her know that you are having difficulty. Take your notes along, and ask your instructor to go over them with you. You may also want to consider using a tape recorder in class, not as a substitute for note-taking, but as a supplement. Continue to take notes as usual, but at the same time record the lecture. When you get behind or miss a point, make a note of where the counter is on the recorder. Later, when you have time, go back to that section on the tape. By doing this, you will be able to fill in any missing information and hopefully clarify any unclear notes.

It may be helpful to share notes with a study partner or study group so you can fill in any information you may have missed. And finally, keep in mind that like any skill, learning to take good notes will require practice. Each semester your note-taking and listening skills will improve.

MEMORY STRATEGIES

An understanding of how memory works and effective ways to use your memory will increase your ability to memorize information. All incoming information enters the **sensory memory**, which holds an exact copy of everything you see or hear for several seconds. On the way to class, you may notice a squirrel in a tree, but you can't recall that experience several moments later. Generally, your sensory memory will hold information just long enough for your **short-term memory** to register it. Short-term memory is the temporary storehouse for information. If your brain does not identify the information as meaningful or important, it quickly disappears. Your short-term memory lets you concentrate on the task at hand, but prevents you from collecting too much information in temporary storage. You are introduced to several people, but can't use their names in talking with them. You did not retain their names beyond sensory memory. Information that your mind identifies as meaningful or important makes its way into **long-term memory**. In order to enter information into your long-term memory, it must be actively processed through your short-term memory. "Active processing" in short-term memory is the key to the successful transfer of information into long-term memory.

Long-term memory can store an unlimited amount of information for long periods of time. Information is stored in long-term memory on the basis of meaning and importance.

what you expect = climate

what you get = weather

Long-term weather

$\mathcal{H}$ = *Highland*

to figure out hemisphere = northern = warm summer months (May/June - Aug/Sep) southern = warm summer months (Oct/Nov - Mar/Apr)

Supplement for Physical Geography
SESSION 5
CLIMATIC CLASSIFICATION

5.1 Climatic classification. The climate classification system used

but, not the only one!

in this course is the most widely-used and accepted climatic

(Köppen)

classification system named after its inventor—Wladimir Koeppen.

"Climatologist"

Trained as a botanist, Koeppen realized that many biological

activities are a function of climatic characteristics. Beginning

with his doctoral dissertation to his death in 1940, he originated,

revised, and refined his classification system. To aid in the

classification of climates, the climatic diagram (called a

climograph) has been developed which displays the variables of

monthly temperature and precipitation on one graphic. The purpose of

any classification system is to make simplicity from complexity;

though the earth/atmospheric energy exchanges with the sun which

create climate variability are extremely complex, we will be simply

concerned with the relationship between potential evaporation and

the amount of moisture received at any geographic location.

5.2 The arctic climates with symbols ET and EF. The E-type climates

are locations where average monthly temperatures are less than 50°

F. Here, precipitation is received, but it comes in the form of snow

and is often not immediately available for biological functions.

E's all less than 50° ET= 32°--50° EF= below

There are two types of E climates; ET (Tundra or Continental

Subarctic) and EF (Ice Cap or Arctic). ET climates have average

temperatures of the warmest month between 50°F and 32°F, and EF

climates are those whose average temperatures of the warmest month

are below 32°F.

A's at equator ---- E's at poles

N. pole

E D C B A

equator

A B C

S. pole

E

no D's in Southern!

Figure 6 Instructor-Provided Class Notes

5.3 The humid-dry boundary. Koeppen rationalized that the two most important climatic variables in determining what type of biological activities would take place in any region are temperature and precipitation. He further reasoned that there is a dynamic relationship between these two variables—the hotter the climate, the more the demand placed on water due to greater evaporative potential. To quantify this relationship, the humid-dry boundary was identified, which marked the difference between a humid and dry climate regime. So, perhaps the first step in an understanding of the classification system is to have a knowledge of the manner in which boundary is calculated. For this purpose, all stations (by definition) receive precipitation evenly distributed throughout the year. This is often not the case, but for reasons of simplicity, the humid-dry boundary will be calculated based on that assumption allowing the use of one equation. The humid-dry boundary for any station with even monthly precipitation distribution is determined by

$$r = 0.44T - 8.w \qquad (1)$$

where r is the rainfall in inches and T the average annual temperature in °F. Therefore, for a location that has an average annual temperature of 50.0°F, the precipitation necessary for a station to be right on the humid-dry boundary is 13.5″ (r = 0.44(50) -8.5). If the station being classified receives more than 13.5″ annually, it has a humid climatic regime; and if the station being classified receives less than 13.5″ at 50°F annual average temperature, it is considered a dry climatic station site and is symbolized with a letter "B."

Information you don't really understand or consider significant will most likely not find its way into long-term memory. This means that your ability to remember what you study depends on your willingness to make sure you thoroughly understand the material and can relate it to existing information in long-term memory.

Organization. Information learned at the knowledge level of Blooms' Taxonomy of thinking and learning is usually memorized. The key to effective memorizing is to organize information in such a way that you can find it easily. The way you organize information will determine how the information is remembered and retrieved. In deciding how to organize information for later recall, you need to ask yourself: "How will I be asked to recall this information?" The answer to this question will determine how you input the information. Memorizing something by rote, means to "regurgitate" the information in the exact same way it is learned. For this type of memorization, you will be able to make use of mnemonic techniques. These techniques serve as a link between the new information and your memory. You have been making many of these links for years, but may not have known that they are called mnemonics.

- *Acronyms* are words created by the first letters of a series of words. For example: FBI, CIA, IRS, USU. By using acronyms, you can create your own cues for recalling a series of facts or words. Be sure to create an acronym that is simple enough to not be forgotten or confused.

- *Acrostics* are creative sentences that help you remember a series of letters that stand for something. You can create acrostics to remember a specific item, such as the planets in our solar system in sequence (Mercury, Venus, Earth, Mars, Jupiter, Saturn, Uranus, Neptune, and Pluto.) Taking the first letter of each word, you would have m, v, e, m, j, s, u, n, and p. Make up a nonsensical phrase to help you remember the exact order, such as, "My very elegant mother just served us nine pies." A good sense of humor will help you remember your sentence.

- *Rhymes and Songs.* Rhymes are used to help remember facts. For example: "In fourteen hundred and ninety-two, Columbus sailed the ocean blue." "Fifty Nifty United States" is an example of a song that helps us to remember many isolated facts, such as the names of all the states.

- *Loci and Peg Systems.* Loci is a strategy where you associate a concept with a place. This includes where you were when you heard the concept, how it looked in your notes, which graphics were on the page containing the information, etc. You can create a visual association between the material to be learned and a familiar place or routine. For instance, suppose you want to learn a list of chemical elements. You choose a familiar route, such as a route across campus. As you pass each building along the way, you assign it a chemical element. Later in your class, you visualize your route. As you "see" each place, you recall the element it represents. The method of loci helps you to remember things in a particular order. This is especially helpful when trying to remember steps in a process. Peg systems work by visualizing pegs or hooks in a closet. You hang information on each peg, and then recall what's on each one.

Mnemonic devices have some limitations. First, the technique is often difficult to learn and remember. You may forget the technique. Second, mnemonic techniques don't work well for remembering technical terms in math and science. And third, mnemonic techniques won't necessarily help you get beyond the knowledge level of thinking. You won't necessarily understand or comprehend the material you are trying to recall.

Association. When asked to recall information that requires that you comprehend and apply the information, you will need to practice effective memory techniques that go beyond rote memorization. The understanding of new material is aided by associating it with other ideas. New information is learned in small related units. These units of knowledge are interrelated with previously learned material. The goal is to establish a chain of relationship and, through related organization, master the new material. The more associations you can create from an idea, the more meaning the new idea will have, and the more likely the material will be retained. Try to associate the information with personal experiences, and see how the information could affect your life. In addition, the more background you have on a subject the easier it is to form these associations and to discern relationships. To gain more background, you may need to reference other textbooks, seek help from your instructor, join a study group, or hire a tutor.

Selection. When trying to remember information, be selective. First, survey what is to be covered. Concentrate on the most significant things to remember. Give most of your attention to that which is new and difficult to understand, yet necessary to remember. Decide on the order of importance, and organize the material into a framework.

Review. Study often. The best review is immediate use of the information. Test yourself by making up illustrations of the material. Use flash cards, outlines, and practice tests to help check your ability to recall the information. Research has demonstrated that a daily short review is likely to increase your success on tests.

Rehearsal. Refresh your memory by allowing time between review sessions. Time between practice sessions allows your mind time to organize and make connections with the new information. Use the rehearsal time to practice using what you have learned. Experiments indicate that the very rapid forgetting, which is so common after a reading session, can be significantly reduced by spaced verbal or written recitation of the material. Rephrase and explain new information to yourself. Talk to someone else or yourself about the topic you've been studying. If you can't explain something, you really haven't learned it.

It is easy to be fooled into believing you know something and then, when asked to recall that piece of information, be unable to do so. For instance, have you ever been reading along in your textbook and come across information that you knew, and therefore skipped it, only to be unable to remember it for a test the next day? You probably did know that information. However, the knowledge you had of it was "recognition knowledge" not "recall knowledge." Recognition knowledge is a surface knowing, a recognizing of certain information as being familiar. Recall or retrieval knowledge is the ability to access that information and to recall it. One way to check whether you have recognition knowledge or retrieval knowledge of a subject is to try to explain that information to someone else. Being able to verbalize new information or to summarize it in writing is usually a sign that you possess sufficient recall knowledge.

Overlearning. Reviewing something that has already been learned sufficiently for still one more time is called overlearning. Anything you can recall instantly without effort has been overlearned. The more important and the more difficult the learning, the more you should reinforce it with frequent practice.

Sleep. Freshly learned material and material that is reviewed is better remembered after a period of sleep than after an equal period of daytime activity when interference may take place. There is some truth to the old adage to "sleep on it." This does not mean placing the textbook under your pillow.

Forgetting. Forgetting is the result of either failing to adequately input information or failing to recall or access the information once it has been input. Often students comment that they got to an exam and "forgot" the information. Unfortunately, their study method may have never put the information beyond a recognition level. Other factors can also affect the input and recall of information. The very nature of memory itself affects the storage of information and its later recall. First, memory is subjective. We tend to remember things that are more favorable to ourselves. The need to feel positive about ourselves causes us to remember things in a positive way (or inversely, in a negative way). Second, memory is interpretive. As we input information into our memory, we interpret and read meaning into the information. Our memory of a fact or an event is then a combination of the original information plus our perceptions and feelings. Third, memory is constructive. We are continually taking bits and pieces of information and putting them together to construct memory. Fourth, memory serves our emotional needs. Stress and emotions can affect memory. Often we remember only what is meaningful to us, or what captures our attention. Competing demands for our attention can interfere with the retrieval of information.

Millions of dollars have been earned by the creators of memory improvement tapes, videos, kits, and workshops. Strategies for increasing the power of your memory can be found on every bookstore shelf. As a student, you will certainly want to develop your memory skills. The ability to accurately recall the information you have read or heard will be vital to your success.

CONCENTRATION

Students often cite lack of concentration as a major barrier to learning information. Some common laments are "I can only concentrate for a few minutes." "Studying is boring." Some common concentration problems include: fatigue, distractions, and poor time management.

Distractions are those things in the environment that compete for attention. These distractions may be external or internal. An inappropriate learning environment will definitely decrease your ability to concentrate. Learning new material requires your complete and focused attention. Being distracted by personal problems and frequent daydreaming divides your attention and causes a decrease in your ability to concentrate.

Concentration strategies. Concentration is giving material your complete and focused attention. This focus is necessary to store information. Without concentration and focus, information is not put into long-term memory for later recall. Often, knowing that we are not concentrating begins a cycle of frustration. "Tomorrow is the test. I don't want to sit here and read this. I can't think at all. I'm going to fail." The fear of failure adds an additional barrier to concentration. Knowing the common causes of poor concentration may help you to focus during your study time. Ineffective time management has a great deal to do with concentration. By setting goals and establishing priorities, you will be better able to schedule time for studying. Procrastination causes stress, which in turn affects your ability to concentrate. Knowing how to pace yourself and prioritize your commitments will directly increase your ability to concentrate.

Barriers to concentration. The major barriers to concentration come under four main categories: distractions, attitude, poor time management, and fatigue. Knowing what is causing your inability to focus may aid you in choosing strategies to solve the problem.

Distractions are those things in the environment that compete for our attention. Minor distractions can be small environmental problems that are simple to control: the phone ringing, the noise of the TV, roommates chattering, the room too hot or too cold, a great view, being hungry, tired, or thirsty. Major distractions absorb your thoughts and are more difficult to manage. Anticipating an upcoming vacation is just as distracting as worrying about relationships or financial problems. Major or minor distractions can make it difficult to remember what you just read in U.S. History.

Strategies to eliminate distractions:

- Be physically prepared to study. Are you sleepy? Hungry?
- Find a place to study that is free of distractions.
- Deal with personal problems before or after studying.
- Write down your problem and set it aside for later.
- Study with a partner to increase motivation.
- Practice increasing your "focused" concentration time. Set a timer and start with short times that will bring you success.
- Practice effective time management strategies, such as creating a study schedule and daily "to do" lists.

Students often confuse "concentration" problems with "interest and attitude" problems. The reality is that not every course will be on a favorite subject. Having a negative attitude about a course creates a concentration barrier. To the extent that you can convince yourself that there is something of interest in each of your classes, you will find that you can concentrate at a higher level. You may have to create a reward system for yourself to overcome an attitude. Rewards can vary from a piece of candy to time with friends, but many students find they work effectively.

Strategies to overcome attitude problems:

- Accept your responsibility for learning the information.
- Accept your instructor's limitations. He/she does not have to "entertain" you.
- Relate the course to your goals. "After this class, I can take a class in my major."
- Break long assignments into smaller parts.

- Set specific study goals for a time block. (For example: finish reading three sections of chapter seven in the history text, or complete two math problems.)
- Study the least interesting subject first.
- Promise yourself a small reward for your concentrated study time.
- Talk about the problem with a friend or professional counselor.

Proper rest, exercise, and nutrition are essential to maintaining a healthy body. Inattention to any of these three areas may result in fatigue and the decreased ability to concentrate. Eat well-balanced meals, include exercise as part of your daily routine, and allow enough time for rest and recreation.

Strategies to prevent fatigue:

- Schedule study times when you are not tired.
- Eat well so you won't be hungry.
- Sign up for a physical education course.
- Exercise with a partner to increase motivation.
- Take advantage of the college exercise facilities.

Causes of poor concentration can also include lack of academic, listening, or note-taking skills. In this text, we list many suggestions to help you in these areas. If you identify your problem area, you can then decide to make changes. Start with a small change. Perhaps you will decide to study longer on a difficult subject. Start with a manageable time to give you success, then increase the time gradually. Be sure to reward yourself for each gain.

WRITING STRATEGIES

Writing to inform. University students will, on the average, write five major papers per school year and many more shorter papers. That's a lot of writing! And every assignment will be different, requiring different kinds of thinking and organization. Regardless of the details of any particular assignment, there are three factors which must always be considered as you begin.

Format. How should the information be presented? Did your professor ask for a one-page critique, an essay that summarizes the positive and negative aspects of a particular topic, a five-page annotated bibliography? If you are unsure about the format for an assignment—ask!

Audience. Obviously your professor will read your assignment, but some students make the mistake of not including enough information because their teacher "already knows everything about it." While this might be true, writing assignments are given not only to encourage your original ideas, but to test your understanding of a subject. Write for your professor, but your writing should be clear enough that any other college student could pick it up and make sense of your ideas, even if he or she were unfamiliar with the assignment itself.

Purpose. Every writing assignment has a purpose. Your job is to understand what that purpose is and then adjust the content and the tone of your paper to meet that purpose. Every writing assignment, from a lab report to a critical analysis of Romeo and Juliet, should make a point. If your writing assignment doesn't make a clear and original point, you should revise it so it does.

Not every writing assignment is the same—know what is expected of you and then write, format, and polish your paper in such a way that your purpose and message are clear. To evaluate the quality and effectiveness of your writing, consider these five criteria:

- Completeness—did you expand on the ideas, or just think superficially about the topic?
- Support—did you back up your ideas and opinions with reasons or proof so that your knowledge of the subject matter is evident? Did you use specific examples, whether from your textbook, lab experiments, class discussion, outside reading, etc.?
- Organization—is your paper easy to read? Is there an adequate introduction and conclusion as well as transitions between parts?
- Authority—does your paper reflect a depth of thought and commitment that a critically thinking student should exhibit? (Do not mistake this for conformity to concepts or ideals that sound good but that you really don't believe in.)
- Correctness—have you proofread your paper sufficiently so that spelling, punctuation, and grammar errors do not interfere with its readability?

The best writing is usually not done in isolation. We all need help generating ideas, organizing our thoughts, or evaluating the effectiveness of our writing.

Writing to learn. Most students think of writing only in terms of completing papers assigned for class. But writing can also be a learning tool; writing to learn can enable you to organize your thinking, increase your understanding, and make personal connections to the material. All of these processes will increase learning and help you remember the material. Below are some ideas for using writing as a tool for learning. These writing activities range from the knowledge/memorization level of thinking to the evaluation level, as discussed in Bloom's Taxonomy of Educational Objectives, and can be adapted to any class—from physics to philosophy to family science.

Keep a class journal. In it you could:

- summarize the main points from lectures in your own words.
- keep a list of questions you need answered.
- write down your goals for that particular class.
- summarize the main ideas in the text chapters.
- summarize sub-sections if the chapters are quite long.
- define terms or concepts in your own words.
- critique the ideas presented in class or the way they are presented by the teacher.

Use writing as a learning activity in study groups or with a study partner. You could:

- exchange chapter or lecture summaries to get a different perspective on the same topic.

- write and exchange sample essay questions and then practice answering them.
- write and exchange sample test questions and then try answering them.

Think up your own ways to use writing to help you learn. Remember, writing isn't just for showing others what you know. It can also be a valuable tool to help you better understand what you know or think or even discover what it is you don't know.

TEST TAKING STRATEGIES

Most course tests measure your ability to remember many facts and figures, as well as your understanding of the course materials. These tests are designed to make you think beyond the knowledge/recognition level of learning. The factors which contribute to good test scores can be summarized in two words: preparation and strategies. Successful preparation for an exam starts at the beginning of each semester and continues throughout. Prepare yourself for higher-level thinking as you study.

Preparation. This activity includes mental and physical readiness.

- *Make a semester study plan.* At the beginning of each semester, develop a daily schedule that allows time for class preparation, study, review, recreation, eating, and sleeping. Be sure you have clearly marked the dates of all exams.
- *Use good review techniques.* Study and review differ from each other. Study refers to learning new material for the first time. Review is critical because it strengthens the retention of new knowledge. Because forgetting takes place most rapidly immediately after learning, it is more effective to review soon after studying or after each class. Your review should include strategies that incorporate the level of thinking required for that class. Do you need to apply the information as well as comprehend the concept? Will you have to solve a problem in your social work class?
  - Review notes and text(s)—list the major concepts that have been covered.
  - Highlight topics that were emphasized in class or on handouts.
  - Concentrate on the vocabulary of the course. Identify words used to represent specific concepts (i.e., the word "mesothermal" in geography) and treat them as you would a foreign language. Make flash cards for drills and try to use these words whenever you review the course materials.
  - Construct diagrams, charts, tables, or lists to summarize relationships.
  - Review and recite often. Try to say or write out complete ideas or facts. Try to be detailed and precise so you are not relying on just recognition of the information when you see the test.
- *Develop a confident attitude.* Your attitude toward exams can make a difference. Tests do serve a good purpose. They give you an opportunity to check your progress. Students who have formed good study habits throughout the semester should be confident.
- *Organize pre-exam hours.* The day before an important exam, plan to review a maximum of three hours, interspersed with pace-changing breaks. Question yourself, recite the main points to yourself, and reread the passages only when you are having

difficulty remembering them. Eat and sleep well to avoid rushing on the morning of the test. Stay calm. Be sure you have all the supplies you need before leaving your room. Arrive on time in order to get a good seat.

- *Attend any study groups.* Sometimes these are a supplement to the course. They can be offered by an instructor—or form a group of your own.

Test preparation also includes finding out what will be covered on the test, what kind of test it will be (i.e., objective, essay, or both), and knowing what you are allowed to bring into the testing room. You learn about these things by asking your professor. If you are afraid or embarrassed to ask during class, then schedule an appointment with him/her to find out this important information.

Test day strategies. Some general strategies for taking tests include:

- *Get off to a good start.* Arrive early for the exam, and sit near the front or in a well-lighted, quiet spot. Avoid friends and panic stricken people. Listen carefully to any instructions.
- *Look over the entire exam.* Pay attention to point values, and figure out a rough time allowance for each section of the exam. Get an idea about what the exam is covering. By reading over the entire exam, you will build confidence in your ability to do well.
- *Read all directions.* Underline all significant words in the directions. Be sure you understand what is asked.
- *Begin to work.* Tackle questions in the order that appeals to you, as this builds confidence. Keep in mind the point values, and use the entire time!
- *Learn to relax.* If you find yourself becoming tense or anxious, stop, take deep breaths, close your eyes, and visualize yourself succeeding. Simple relaxation exercises such as flexing and relaxing your muscles will help relieve your stress.
- *Learn from the test.* Go over the test results, and use the information to help you prepare more adequately for the next exam.

Each type of test requires different test-taking skills. It is wise to be aware of reasons students have difficulty with these tests and the strategies for success.

The multiple choice test. Students typically have a difficult time with taking multiple choice tests. Some reasons for this are:

- Imprecise knowledge.
- Incomplete or sloppy reading of the question.
- Limited ways to trigger memory.

Imprecise knowledge. Because students often study by "looking over" the material, rather than actively processing, they have an imprecise memory of its meaning (recognition knowledge vs. recall knowledge). Although multiple choice questions are used most often to test your memory of details, facts, and relationships, they are also used to test your comprehension and your ability to solve problems or the application and analysis learning levels. Students are easily confused by the choices or alternative answers. Some ways to counter this problem are to make up practice tests, make study notes, use 3 x 5 cards, and review daily. Also discuss the concepts with a study partner or study group. Attempting to verbalize the information in your own words increases your comprehension level and the ability to recall the information. The Developing Study Guide Questions (Exercise 6) allows you the opportunity to decide what level of knowledge of information is required to answer test questions in your courses.

Incomplete or sloppy reading of the question or item. If you don't know what decision you are asked to make about the topic, it will be hard to select the correct answer. Some students read questions without attention or without thinking, and jump to the alternative choices without really knowing what has been asked. When you wind up trying to find the correct answer without really knowing what was asked, you can become confused. Sometimes the choices which you are given muddle your thinking. The following suggestion may be useful. Read the question or the item as if it were an independent free-standing statement. Do not look at answers. Think of the answer. Only then should you look for a MATCH among the given answers. READ . . . THINK . . . MATCH. For example:

"Horse" is to "animal" as "ivy" is to _____.

Stop! Think of the answer! Then find a match to your thoughts.

Limited ways to trigger memory. Some students study by using one word to act as a cue to the memory. If the professor doesn't use this word in the test question, these students are lost. Without that limited one word, they cannot find the information in memory. If students have stayed at the knowledge or recognition level of learning, by reciting the answer using textbook words or the exact words used by the professor instead of thinking about the meaning and relationship of the ideas, then different wording in the answer may not result in recall.

Expand your cues to trigger memory by studying for understanding. Try to explain what you have learned by using your own words (but check to ensure your own words are accurate). Go over your notes and practice questions and substitute synonyms wherever possible.

Students often ask: "What if I read the question carefully and find no match among the alternative answers?" Then GUESS! The following suggestions are helpful hints for educated guessing and eliminating some of the options.

- If two answers are similar, except for one or two words, choose one of these answers.
- If two answers have similar sounding or looking words, choose one of these.
- Look for answers that are grammatically correct.
- If two quantities are equal, choose one of them.
- If there is a wide range, choose a middle value.
- Look for root words in the answers that are similar to words in the item or the question.
- Look for answers within the test itself.
- Out for words like *always*, *never*, and *only*. They must be interpreted as meaning all of the time, not just 99% of the time. These choices are frequently incorrect.

The essay exam. The other type of exam that some students have problems with is the essay exam. Preparation for an essay test, as for any test, requires close and careful review, and possible rereading of textbooks and class notes. Many professors will announce in advance the general area the test will cover, the concepts, issues, controversies, theories, etc. Reviewing your lecture notes will also reveal which broad areas have been central to class discussion and are therefore likely to appear on the test. The following suggestions may be helpful in preparing for an essay exam.

Anticipation. Anticipate questions that are likely to be on the test. Use previous tests and your class notes as your basic source material for this task. Ask yourself, "What are the concepts and relationships involved in the material?" Review notes, omitting detail. Review major headings and chapter summaries in the text.

Condensation. Organize all of your material into principle groups. Identify the major concepts, the main subordinate concepts under each one, and the critical details. Now, summarize the material in your own words. Boil down the material to a rather tight outline form. Fit the necessary details into the concepts.

Practice. Some students profit by making up sample questions and then practicing answering them. It is important to note that mastery of a course's special vocabulary is essential groundwork. You will frequently be required to manipulate terminology. Getting this done is like tying your shoes before running. Failure to do it will most likely weaken your performance. So practice using the vocabulary of the course by making flash cards and keeping word lists.

Strategies for the completion of the essay exam. Having a plan for taking an essay test will help you with the organized thinking that is required.

- Read the directions carefully. Notice whether you must answer all essay questions or whether you may choose which ones to answer.

- Read every question before beginning—clarify any unclear questions. Select those questions for which you are best prepared, and begin with the easiest one. This will score quick points for you, inspire confidence, and promote clear thinking. It will also enable you to avoid content overlap by making you aware of information that could be better used in answering another question. After each answer, leave enough space to add further ideas that may come to mind as the exam proceeds.

- Make a "brain dump." Jot notes alongside each question. Quickly (in about 5 minutes) note a few key words and phrases alongside each question. List technical terms and names that are right on the tip of your tongue. This will keep them available later, when pressures and anxiety may otherwise block them off.

- Calculate and budget time for each question. Budget time according to the point value of each question. Questions worth more points should be given more time.

- Answer the easy questions first. These are the questions you are certain you can answer correctly. This develops a confident attitude and helps you feel more at ease. After each answer, leave enough space to add further ideas that may come to mind as the exam proceeds.

- Don't get bogged down. Do not hesitate too long on a difficult question. Inaction may block your thinking. Forcing yourself to write increases your chances of recalling the answer. "Free association" or freely jotting down on a piece of scrap paper words that come to mind as you think about the answer may help you overcome blocking and remind you of new ideas to be organized into your answer.

Essay exam key words. When thinking about the content of your essay, remember to note the key instruction words. In answering an essay question, you want to be sure that you are answering the question that has been asked, and not the question which you think has been asked. The Essay Exam Key Word (Exercise 7) asks you to apply your knowledge of clue words to practice essay test questions.

The words in Figure 7 are commonly found in essay test questions. Understanding them is essential to success in answering such questions. If you want to do well on essay tests, then study this page thoroughly. Know these words backwards and forwards. To heighten your awareness of them, underline the words when you see them in a test question.

Before you even begin to write, you should make a skeletal outline. This is not a "doodle." It is a brief, informative summary of the information which you will cover in your answer. It will save you time and stress by providing direction and helping you avoid repetition. In addition, if you don't have time to finish, you can include your outline and maybe gain some partial credit.

Your instructor is greatly influenced by the compactness and clarity of an organized answer. To begin writing in hopes that the right answer will somehow turn up is time consuming and usually futile. To know a little and present it well is, by and large, superior to knowing much and presenting it poorly. Therefore, be concise and to the point. Think more and write less. Avoid flowery language. Instructors are usually impressed by directness, brevity, conciseness, organization, and accuracy.

A common problem that students have in writing short-answer and essay exams is in being direct. One mark of a good answer is directness in responding to the question. In a sociology course, the essay question may ask you to "describe the major differences between patrilineal, matrilineal, and bilateral societies." You answer the question directly and forcefully in the first sentence. "The major differences between the patrilineal, matrilineal, and bilateral societies are. . . ." Expand your first sentence according to your skeletal outline, supporting the main idea with facts, illustrations, and reasons, using the technical terms and references from your textbooks and lectures.

In conclusion, writing essay answers may take practice. Be sure to reread your corrected test and learn from the comments written by the instructor. Keep the following points in mind as you develop this skill.

- *Always write something.* If you do not know the answer to a question, try to reason it out. Sometimes, just getting your thoughts on paper will help you make connections with the ideas. You may get partial credit; you will never get credit for empty space.
- *Summarize and conclude.* The introduction will be the "thesis" or the main point to be made. The summary is simply a rephrasing of the introduction.

Essay Exam Word	Answer should:
Analyze	Break into several parts; and discuss, examine, or interpret each part.
Compare	Examine two or more things. Identify similarities and differences.
Contrast	Show differences. Set in opposition.
Criticize	Make judgments. Evaluate comparative worth. Criticism often involves analysis.
Define	Give the meaning; usually a meaning specific to the course or subject determine the precise limits of the term to be defined.
Describe	Give a detailed account. Make a picture with words. List characteristics, qualities, and parts.
Discuss	Consider and debate or argue the pros and cons of an issue. Write about a conflict.
Enumerate	List several ideas, aspects, events, things, qualities, reasons, etc.
Explain	Make an idea clear. Show logically how a concept is developed. Give the reasons for an event.
Evaluate	Give your opinion or cite the opinion of an expert. Include evidence to support the evaluation.
Illustrate	Give concrete examples. Explain clearly by using comparisons or examples.
Interpret	Comment upon, give examples, describe relationships. Explain the meaning. Describe, then evaluate.
Outline	Describe main ideas, characteristics, or events. (Does not necessarily mean—"write a Roman numeral/letter outline.")
Prove	Support with facts (especially facts presented in class or in the text.)
Relate	Show the connections between ideas or events. Provide a larger context.
State	Explain precisely.
Summarize	Give brief, condensed account. Include conclusions. Avoid unnecessary details.
Trace	Show the order of events or progress of a subject or event.

Figure 7 Essay Exam Key Words

- *Be sure you leave enough time to reread your answer.* Check your answer and correct any errors in spelling, grammar, sentence structure, or penmanship. Be sure you haven't left out any words, parts of words, or parts of answers.

TEST ANXIETY

Test anxiety has two components: a mental component and a physical component. The mental component consists of your beliefs, ideas, and concerns regarding exams. The physical component includes a variety of physical symptoms: tightening of the neck/back muscles, sweating, increased heart rate, increased blood pressure, feelings of irritability and frustration, shaking hands, stomachache, or headache. The list goes on. Fifteen to twenty-five percent of all students suffer moderate cases of test anxiety. A little bit of anxiety may be necessary to motivate you to do well. The difference between test anxious and non-test anxious students is in their focus. Non-test anxious students think only about the exam and getting it done. They are extremely well focused on the task of taking the exam. Test-anxious students perform badly, because their attention is not focused solely on the exam. Test-anxious students divert their attention from the exam to the mental and physical sensations which they are experiencing.

It is accurate to say that too little anxiety inhibits performance, and too much hinders it. As with many stress-related conditions, the causes are varied: parents and teachers expecting too much, fear of failure, feeling of having to please others, fear of not getting accepted to certain schools or programs, fear of damaging an academic record, or having a perfectionistic attitude. Anxiety is learned; it grows and snowballs as students push themselves and try harder. Students who find themselves dealing with intense feelings of anxiety and worry need to seek help.

Most students who work to eliminate test anxiety are very successful. A word of caution. Test anxiety is not the same as **test stupidity**! If you have missed class, not taken notes, neglected to read the text, didn't have time to study—you are not anxious—you are underprepared! Don't confuse inadequate preparation, and the normal anxiety that accompanies it, with the irrational fear that many students have about taking tests.

"I FORGOT!" The jolt of going "blank" on a test can raise beads of perspiration on the most experienced test taker. It happens. The term or idea, which you knew minutes before the test, is suddenly locked tight in your memory. During the exam, if you blank out, don't fight it, accept it. Shrug it off, and go on with the test. Otherwise, your anxiety increases and absorbs all of your attention. If instead, you switch your attention to other questions, your memory will continue to search for the answer automatically. With less anxiety, you may recall the answer before the end of the test, instead of 12 hours later!

When you return to the skipped items, think methodically. Systematically search for your memory of them. Pay attention to key words in the question, and recall synonyms for them. Losing something in your memory is like losing your car keys. Ask questions of yourself that lead you to the lost memory, just like you ask questions that lead you to the lost set of car keys.

COLLEGE READING STRATEGIES

You may have arrived on campus feeling confident in your academic reading skills. Having a reading section in this book may appear unnecessary to you. Reading in your high school courses may have varied, from being able to pass the class without looking at the text, to required reading of several texts, novels, or supplemental readings. You may have heard rumors that college reading is "different," however, the only problem you currently anticipate is the expense of the text.

Often, by mid-semester, students realize why college reading may require more skills than they previously had to demonstrate. There are active study/reading approaches to textbooks that will involve you in using your textbooks to gain information. College classes usually require a text, often expensive, and reading assignments that must be completed in order to pass the class. You may find the text difficult to comprehend. The reading assignments contain more facts and ideas per page and are written at a higher reading level than high school texts. In fifteen weeks, you may have to be responsible for the amount of information you covered in an entire year in high school. Figure 8 lists common reading problems and suggested study strategies to help you with this area.

Active study reading is not "speed-reading." Research has shown that speed-reading is only effective when you are reading information that you already know and understand. What students do need are active reading/study strategies and a flexible reading rate. In some instances, you will be able to speed up your reading, but often new information requires more than one reading and an interactive approach. Active reading strategies involve you in the reading process, so that you are able to effectively read and comprehend the material in the textbook. With the use of time management skills, concentration techniques, and study strategies, you can feel in charge of all the reading required in college.

What affects reading comprehension? At the beginning of this chapter, you were introduced to the strategy of PBID to check your academic readiness. Similarly, you should check your readiness to comprehend textbook material by identifying your **Purpose, Background, Interest, and Difficulty (PBID)**. Assessing yourself in each area, then developing strategies to improve each area, will help you read effectively. You will be able to recall and use the information from the textbook.

Purpose. Students often sit down to read with only the thought that they have to "study" this chapter and hopefully retain "something." Take a minute to identify the purpose of the reading, that is, what is your reason for reading the textbook? Textbooks are read for different reasons:

- To build background knowledge so you can understand the lecture.
- To add supplemental information to your class notes.
- To learn details, such as the classification of types of rock or the time sequence of events that led up to the Civil War.
- To be prepared for a class discussion: the causes of the Civil War and the effect it had on the future politics of the South.
- To understand principles, processes, and concepts, such as Mendel's Law of Genetics, Newton's Three Laws of Motion, or the properties of real numbers.

Causes of Reading Problems	Active Reading Strategies
1. Lack of motivation.	• Evaluate your reading purpose, your background knowledge, your interest in the material, and the difficulty of the reading. • Do the most difficult reading first. • Arrange your schedule so that you read at your most productive study time. • Find a way to personalize the information. • Join a study group, divide the reading responsibility so that each person creates a summary and study guide for the group.
2. Lack of background knowledge and understanding of the subject.	• Skim the chapter headings, pictures, charts, graphs, and diagrams. • Read the summary or conclusion first. • Get a tutor to explain difficult concepts. • Form a study group to discuss topics. • Allow additional time to reread the text 2–3 times.
3. Inability to concentrate.	• Formulate a purpose for reading. • Practice a study strategy such as SQ3R. • Annotate the text. • Look for signal words to follow the organization of the text. • Break the reading time into manageable blocks.
4. Frustration with inability to recall the information.	• Make connections between old and new information. • Review the main concepts daily. • Create study guides that reflect the type of test for that class.
5. Course and textbook contain difficult vocabulary and terminology.	• Make a course vocabulary notebook or 3x5 card system, listing new words and definitions. • Review the vocabulary daily. • Learn common prefixes, suffixes, and root words to help you build your vocabulary. • Use color to highlight similarities and differences in word parts.

Figure 8 Reading Comprehension Problems and Strategies

How do you know the purpose of the text for each class?

1. Read the syllabus, and pay careful attention to the relationship between the reading assignments and the class topics.
2. Talk to the instructor.
3. Talk to other students who have had the class or are in class with you. Find out how they used, or are using, the text for the class.

Background. Your reading comprehension is strongly affected by your background knowledge or what you already know about the subject. This is why:

*   If you have high knowledge of the subject, it may be easier for you to read the material. You will be able to meet your purpose quicker than if the information is totally new to you.
*   If your knowledge of the subject is low, you will have to build up your knowledge base. Some lectures are intended to build background before attempting textbook reading. However, you will often be expected to do this on your own. Time management becomes a factor, as you may have to reread your text three times to build up enough knowledge to comprehend the information.

How do you check your background for reading?

1. Before reading the chapter, skim the chapter headings, pictures, charts, graphs, and diagrams.
2. Read the summary and think about what you know about the subject.
3. Read the syllabus, and mark the topics that you know something about.
4. Review your notes, and look for connections between the lecture and the reading.
5. Discuss new information with other students in a study group. This will enhance your knowledge base and help you comprehend the information.

Interest. Students often complain that they don't like to read the text because it is not interesting. In many cases this is a true statement, but it doesn't remove the fact that in many classes, if you do not read the text, you will not pass the class. If you avoid the text because of lack of interest, then you need to take some action to make the reading bearable for that semester.

How do you create interest in what you need to read?

1. Break your reading session into small time units: twenty minutes of concentrated reading, then a small break, then twenty minutes more of focused reading.
2. Create questions before you read. Pretend they are real test questions, and you must know the answers to pass the class.
3. Use a specific reading strategy, such as SQ3R, to keep focused.
4. Do something with the information as you read the text. Write lists or notes in the margins. Create a picture of the information in your mind. Write an outline or draw pictures of the process.

5. Share the reading with study partners. Divide up the chapter into sections, and make each student responsible for reading and teaching the concepts from their section to the other members of the group. Be aware that the section you learn best will be the one that you teach.

6. Talk to the instructor and ask questions about the subject matter. Ask him/her for advice about how to read and comprehend the text. The instructor may say something to spark your interest.

7. Reward yourself for reading and studying material that is not interesting to you.

Difficulty. The difficulty of the reading material can encourage or discourage a student from reading and studying the text. Sometimes the format of the text is more difficult than the actual course material. You have little control over the choice of the text, but you do have options if the reading is difficult.

How do you cope with difficult reading material?

1. Think again about your purpose for reading, your prior knowledge of the subject, and your interest in the course and material. Are any of these factors making the reading difficult? Reread the suggestions in this section and the reading solutions chart in Figure 8.

2. Get a tutor for the class or attend group study sessions. At these sessions, difficult information is explained and discussed. This may make the reading less complex and more interesting.

3. Read another text that is on the same subject, but is written in a different style or at a different reading level. You can check out textbooks at the library.

The SQ3R Reading Strategy. After you have evaluated your purpose, background, interest, and difficulty, then you are ready to begin the reading/study session. Just as when you begin a journey to a new destination, you follow a map or plan, so should your reading session have a plan. SQ3R is a basic reading system that is often used by college students to improve their reading and studying.

How Do I Use SQ3R?

S = Survey. (Gather the information necessary to focus and formulate reading goals.)

• Read the title, headings, and subheadings of the chapter or the article. This helps your mind prepare to receive the information.

• Read the introduction and summary to get an overview of the main ideas. This will familiarize you with the concepts and how the chapter fits the author's purposes.

• Notice the graphics—charts, maps, diagrams, etc. are there to make a point—don't miss them.

• Pay attention to reading aids—italics, bold face print, chapter objectives, and end-of-chapter questions are all included to help you sort, comprehend, and remember information.

Q = Question. (Question as you survey. This helps your mind engage and concentrate as you actively search for answers to questions.)

- Ask yourself what YOU already know about the subject.
- As you read each of the above parts, ask yourself what is meant by the title, headings, subheadings, and captions. One section at a time, turn the bold face headings into as many questions as you think will be answered in that section. Write these down on 3 x 5 cards or create a study guide.
- Add further questions as you proceed through the section.
- Ask yourself, "What did the instructor say about the assignment in class? What handouts support the reading? What is the purpose of the reading assignment?"

R = Read. (Read and think actively. Fill in the information around the questions and structure you have been building.)

- Look for main ideas and supporting details. Use outlining, underlining, and text-marking skills. Read to answer the questions that were raised in the question step.
- Read carefully all of the underlined, italicized, and bold face words or phrases.

R = Recite. (Recite right after reading an assignment. This trains your mind to concentrate and learn as it reads.)

- Use good judgment about places to stop and recite.
- Use outlining and underlining skills. (Do not underline long passages. Use a pencil to first underline important information. Only mark after you have read a passage AND understood it.)
- Write a summary statement of each section.
- Quiz yourself on the main points. See if you can answer from memory. If not, look back again, and don't go on to the next section until you can recite.
- Connect new material with what you already know about the subject.
- Write questions about any material you do not understand, and ask your instructor to explain it.
- Write the answers to the questions you created.

R = Review. (Review after you recite: daily, weekly, and before a test. This refines your mental organization and puts information into long-term memory.)

- Look over your outlines, underlining, and any notations you made in your textbook.
- Recite briefly the main ideas to keep the information fresh in your mind.
- Make practice test questions from review notes.
- Relate the textbook information to the Levels of Knowledge in Bloom's Taxonomy. Can you use the information beyond the basic knowledge level?

How to adapt the SQ3R Study System. There is not one study system that works for everyone all the time. Finding a study system that helps you read, understand, and remember the information depends on many factors that have been discussed in this book. For each class, you will have concepts to learn that are presented in distinct formats. Your commitment to identify the concepts, then create and practice a study system you choose, is more important than the type of system used.

When creating a study system, SQ3R can be a starting point. You can then adapt the steps to fit the concepts in the class and your preferred way to learn. Your system may include outside resources, such as a tutor or study group. Figure 9 summarizes suggested ways to adapt your study system.

Using signal words and phrases. Signal words can help you understand relationships between ideas. They can guide you through a textbook passage, showing where you need to concentrate more, or where you may speed up on your reading. The words will help you anticipate where the author will lead the discussion. If you observe the words carefully, they can be a useful tool in marking a text for main ideas. Figure 10 lists some commonly used signal words and their meanings in a textbook pattern.

Read the following paragraph. As you read, identify each signal word and think about its meaning in the sentence. How does the word guide you in following the author's thoughts? What do you think will be the main subject of the next paragraph?

*"**Geography is what geographers do.**" This statement by A.E. Parkins is an effort to define the discipline of geography. The word geography comes from Greek "geo" meaning "earth" and "graphicus" meaning "to write a descrip-*

Course	Concepts	Study System May Include:
Social Sciences	Major theorists in the field. Theories and principles of behavior.	Underlining and marking as you read. Making charts to compare theories. Attending SI sessions.
Foreign Languages	Vocabulary words, meanings, pronunciations, and tenses.	Practicing translation and pronunciation at the language lab. Adding flash cards and conjugation charts to your review step.
Literature	Elements of writing: plot, characters, point of view, theme, style, and tone.	Interpreting, evaluating, and writing about the selection.
Math	Formulas to learn, Sample problems and exercises.	Practice for solving problems; a math tutor.

Figure 9 Adapt the SQ3R Study System

1. **Example Words: To indicate that another point or an example follows:**

to illustrate	for example	for instance	another
also	furthermore	moreover	specifically
such as			

2. **Emphasis Words: To indicate that the next information is important:**

most important	remember that	pay attention to	above all
a key idea	the main point	most significant	of primary concern

3. **Cause and Effect Words: Check to be sure you know the cause for each effect word:**

because	since	due to	consequently
as a result	effect	cause	for
accordingly	if . . . . then	therefore	thus, so

4. **Summary Words: To indicate that a conclusion follows:**

therefore	finally	consequently	in conclusion
so	to conclude	in a nutshell	to sum up

5. **Time Words: To indicate that a time relationship is being established:**

numbers	steps	stages	next
finally	first, second, etc.	the four steps . . .	

6. **Compare/contrast Words: To indicate concepts are to be looked at from more than one angle:**

similar	like	disadvantages	different
pros and cons	in contrast	equally	contrary to
conversely	on the other hand		

7. **Swivel Words: To indicate an exception to a stated fact:**

however	although	but	nevertheless
though	except	yet	still

Figure 10 Signal Words for Note-Taking and Reading

tion." Geography, therefore, deals with descriptions of the earth, especially how space is occupied on our earth. It is concerned with the investigation of spatial variations of people, places, things, or any other observable phenomena on earth. As a discipline, geography is divided into two main areas of focus, i.e., human and physical. Human geography is concerned with global cultures, histories, economics, and politics, to name a few areas of study. Physical *geography, on the other hand, deals with the interrelations of the atmosphere, hydrosphere, biospheres, and lithosphere. Due to the vastness of each of these natural spheres, it is helpful for the physical geographer to have a working knowledge of scientific notation.*

Reading and marking textbooks. When you read a chapter in a textbook, the quickest way to focus on the information that you need to learn is to mark the information. Information that is marked in an organized format will be learned in an organized manner. You may have mastered the use of colored highlighters to mark information, but that doesn't organize the information for later study and review.

Annotate means to add marks. By using a system of symbols and notation, not just colored highlighters, you mark the text after the first reading so that a complete rereading will not be necessary. The marking should include important points that you will need to review for an exam.

When should you annotate your text? Annotating should be done after a unit of thought has been presented, when the information can be viewed as a whole. This may mean marking after only one paragraph or after three pages, as what you mark will depend a great deal on your purpose, background, interest and the difficulty of the text. If you mark as you read, too much may be marked and you may be unable to see the "big picture" or main concepts. It takes time for the brain to organize information; so if you read, think, and then mark, the main points will develop and you can decide what you need to mark to remember later.

How do you annotate your text? These signals should be marked:

- Underline all the headings, key terms, and definitions.
- Add important information to illustrations. Explanations are usually given on the same page as the illustrations. Write your title near the illustration.
- Highlight or underline important people, dates, or time sequences.
- Turn the heading into a question by writing a question phrase in front of the heading. Use who, how, why, what, or when to start your question.
- Read the section to find the answer to your question.
- Underline or circle the answer. In the margin, write ANS and a few words to answer the question. Most texts are dense with facts and dates and there may be several parts of the answer to your question. Mark and number each part that answers your question.

To mark terms and definitions: Note how your text prints key terms. They are usually printed in italics or bold, but the definitions that follow appear in regular print.

- Underline or circle a key term and its definition.
- In the margin, write the key terms.
- If the key term is also an answer to a question, write ANS above the words in the margin.

To mark important information signaled by lists:

- Circle the words that tell you what a list is about.
- the items in the list, if they do not already have numbers and letters.
- In the margin, write what the list is about in a word or two. Then, list the points in an abbreviated format.
- If the list is also an answer to your question phrase, write ANS in the margin next to the words which introduce the list.

Figure 6 shows an example of an annotated page.

NAME: _____ **DATE:** _____

EXERCISE 4. NOTE-TAKING: CORNELL METHOD

What you are expected to do: Use the *Cornell Method* of note-taking during one lecture in a course. (See Figure 5.)

Before class: Get prepared.

- Complete any reading or written assignments.

During class: Use good listening and notetaking techniques.

- Sit as close to the front as possible.
- Listen for signal words and watch for cues from the instructor for important information.
- Concentrate on the lecture.
- Ask questions if applicable.
- Record notes from the lecture in the right-hand column of your sectioned paper.
- Use chapter notes to assist with note-taking if applicable.

After class:

- Edit your notes and then reduce them within 24 hours. Use the recall column of your sectioned paper. Then summarize your notes.
- Recite (aloud) the answers or information triggered by the key terms, questions, or statements that you have written in the recall column.
- Review your notes (using the recall column) at least once before turning in this assignment.
- Comment on this experience: What worked, what didn't, how can you improve the process for yourself?

What you are expected to submit: Submit a photocopy of your notes. Remember: The notes must be done using the Cornell Method of note-taking.

This assignment is due on _____.

NAME: _____ **DATE:** _____

EXERCISE 5. NOTE-TAKING: PREPARED NOTES

What you are expected to do: Using prepared notes from one of your courses, annotate and summarize notes for further study. (See Figure 6.)

Before class: Get prepared.

- Complete any reading or written assignments.
- Read the prepared notes.

During class: Use good listening and note-taking techniques.

- Sit as close to the front as possible.
- Concentrate on the lecture.
- Ask questions if applicable.
- Mark notes from the lecture, underlining, adding examples, marking questions or confusing concepts.
- Use chapter notes to assist with note-taking if applicable.

After class:

- Summarize your notes at the end of the section.
- Recite the information orally or create an additional study guide.
- Review your notes at least once before turning in this assignment.
- Comment on this exercise: What helped, what do you need to do to improve the effectiveness of your note-taking annotations?

What you are expected to submit: Submit a photocopy of your notes. Remember: The notes must demonstrate additional information from the lecture.

This assignment is due on _____.

EXERCISE 6. DEVELOPING STUDY GUIDE QUESTIONS

Use a class you are taking this semester, and choose material that you will be expected to know for an upcoming test. The material can be from lecture notes, required textbook reading, articles, etc. Prepare six test questions on the class material, one from each of the six learning levels. (*Note: Use "Definition and Examples for the Six Thinking/Learning Levels" in Figure 4 to help you develop test questions.*)

Name of Class: _____

Knowledge-level question:

   What makes this a knowledge-level question?

Comprehension-level question:

   What makes this a comprehension-level question?

Application-level question:

   What makes this an application-level question?

Analysis-level question:

   What makes this an analysis-level question?

Synthesis-level question:

   What makes this a synthesis-level question?

Evaluation-level question:

   What makes this an evaluation-level question?

EXERCISE 7. ESSAY EXAM KEY WORDS

See Figure 7, Essay Exam Key Words, for definitions.

1.   Test your knowledge of essay exam key words by matching terms to definitions.

   a.   analyze   _____   to support or deny by showing evidence or facts.

   b.   criticize   _____   break into parts and explain parts and their importance.

   c.   trace   _____   to make clear or comprehensible.

   d.   evaluate   _____   to show the order of events or development.

   e.   prove   _____   list several ideas, events, aspects, etc., briefly.

   f.   enumerate   _____   to point out both good and bad characteristics.

   g.   explain   _____   to point out both good and bad features, along with a statement or comment or opinion.

   h.   summarize   _____   report various sides of an issue and relationships between points.

   i.   discuss   _____   point out characteristics two or more items have in common and their differences.

   j.   outline   _____   present main points and major subpoints in an organized fashion.

   k.   interpret   _____   present main point in general sentences.

   l.   compare   _____   explain by using examples or demonstrations.

NAME: _____   DATE: _____

EXERCISE 8. PRACTICE USING SQ3R

Directions: The following exercise is designed to give you practice in the steps of SQ3R.

Section I. Survey

1. Name of textbook:

2. List at least two questions or thoughts which the title suggests to you:

    _____

    _____

3. List at least two major points the author makes in the Preface:

    _____

    _____

4. List at least two major points the author makes in the Introduction:

    _____

    _____

5. Take at least three chapter titles listed in the Table of Contents and turn them into questions:

    _____

    _____

    _____

6. If there is an Appendix, what does it contain?

    _____

7. Does the book contain a Glossary? Yes _____ No _____ An Index? Yes _____ No _____ If the answers are yes, look over the Glossary and/or thumb through the Index looking for familiar names, places, or terms. How much do you think you are going to know about the contents?

8. Look through the first two chapters of the book and check any of the following aids used in them.

    ___ headings   ____ footnotes   ___ pictures

    ___ subheadings   ____ bibliography   ___ graphs

    ___ italics   ____ study questions   ___ bold vocabulary words

    ___ summary   ____ assignments   ___ other

Section II. Question

Use the textbook you surveyed. Pick one chapter.

Title of Chapter: _____

1. What do you think is the main idea of the chapter?

    _____

    _____

2. Turn three headings into questions.

    _____

    _____

    _____

3. Write the answer to one of the questions in your own words. Use a format that will help you remember the information: an outline, list, drawing, diagram, etc.

    _____

    _____

    _____

Section III. Read, Recite, Review

Now, think about how you will actively **Read** the text, **Recite** the information, and **Review** the material.

1. Describe your active reading techniques. (Did you annotate, answer questions, etc.?)

    _____

    _____

2. Describe what you will do when you review the material. (Will you create an outline, study sheets, study cards, etc.?)

    _____

    _____

3. Attach a photocopy of a page from your textbook and show how you annotated the important information.

Chapter 4

Evaluating Information Sources

This is the best book ever written by any man on the wrong side of a question of which he is profoundly ignorant.

—THOMAS B. MACAULAY

INTRODUCTION

Never before has there been so much information available or so many ways to disseminate and retrieve it. Even as you read this, Web sites are being created, books and newspapers are being published, and new ways of storing and retrieving information are being developed. Many have characterized what is happening as "information overload." As someone looking for information, you will need to know not only how to locate information, but also how to evaluate the information that you locate. You will find that not all information sources are suitable for your research; nor is all information reliable.

How critical are you?

- Can you tell if the information is reliable?
- Can you tell the difference between propaganda and fact?
- Can you spot a hoax?
- Can you determine whether an author is qualified to write on this subject?

Confronted with the wide array of print, electronic, oral, and visual resources available, you need to be able to make independent judgments about the suitability and the quality of the sources you locate. This chapter will provide you with criteria for selecting appropriate material and evaluating the material you find.

APPLYING EVALUATION CRITERIA

As you locate sources of information cast a critical eye on the content. Are the sources reliable, fair, objective, lacking hidden motives?

The ability to determine the suitability and worth of a particular source is one of the most important research skills you can acquire. It is also one of the most difficult because you are dealing primarily with unknowns. The task is further complicated by the fact that there are so many different formats to deal with—books, periodicals, reference books, CD-ROM and DVD, and Internet resources. Most of the books and periodicals that you find in the library have already undergone some evaluative measures. Publishers edit books and periodicals; articles in scholarly journals are "refereed" by peers in the field; librarians employ evaluative techniques in selecting materials for their collections. Information on the Internet, on the other hand, has not undergone any such selection process, so you will have to be especially vigilant when you use information found on the Internet. There is no single test that you can apply to determine whether a work is reliable or whether the contents are accurate or truthful. Instead, you must make a judgment based on a number of clues or indicators.

Table 1 is a set of criteria together with questions and discussion that can serve as a checklist to help you evaluate books, periodical articles, or other information that you locate.

EVALUATING INTERNET SOURCES

Unlike resources such as magazines, journals, and books that are subjected to some type of selection process (editing, peer review, library selection), most information on the Internet is almost totally lacking in quality control. The onus rests with the user to determine the quality and reliability of information on the Internet. In any information that is posted on the Web there are some telltale signs that should lead you to suspect the credibility of the information: poor grammar, misspelling, or inflammatory words. Beyond the obvious things you should also be able to apply some criteria to determine the quality of a work. Some of the same criteria that are listed in Table 1 can be used to evaluate Internet resources; however, because of the unique nature of information on the Internet, you need to apply a slightly different checklist (see Table 2).

EVALUATIVE REVIEWS

You may be able to locate critical reviews of books in a reviewing source, such as *Book Review Index* or *Book Review Digest*. Book reviews may provide a more in-depth analysis than one you are able to make by applying the criteria in Table 1. Book reviews may appear in journals dedicated solely to reviewing books, or they may appear in subject-based professional journals. Book reviews help answer such questions as whether the book makes a valuable contribution to the field, contains accurate information, or is overly biased or controversial. Articles in scholarly journals are refereed: that is, the authors' peers in the field have subjected them to critical review before publication. Many of the online databases will indicate whether or not a journal is refereed.

Evaluations of Web sites appear in many journals and magazines and in Internet rating services. Many Web pages list all of the awards they have won. For example, the page entitled "All the Virology on the WWW" has a separate page listing all of the awards it has received (http://www.virology.net/ATVaward.html). The author of this page claims to be the "single site for virology information on the Internet." The list of reviews as well as awards will help you determine whether the claim is mere hyperbole or if this is, indeed, the best source for information on virology.

Table 1	**EVALUATING INFORMATION SOURCES**

AUTHORITATIVENESS

Author

- What are the author's education, training, and level of expertise or experience in the field?

    Look for biographical information, the author's title, employment, position, and institutional affiliation.

- Are there other works in the same field by this author?

    Check the online catalog and databases on the same subject.

- What is the author's reputation or standing among peers?

    If a journal article, check to see if it is a refereed journal, i.e., the articles have been subjected to a critical evaluation by one or more experts in the field.

    If a signed article in a subject encyclopedia, read the preface to see how authors were selected.

- If the author is a corporation or an agency, is it one that is well known in the field?

Publisher

- Is the publisher well known in the field?

- Are there many works published by this publisher?

    Check the online catalog to find other books by the publisher.

- Does a university press publish the source?
- Is the publisher a professional organization?

    Generally one can assume that reputable publishers, professional associations, or university presses will publish high quality materials.

COMPREHENSIVENESS

- Are all aspects of the subject covered or have obvious facts been omitted?

    Examine the table of contents of books or peruse the article or Web source.

- Does the work update other sources or does it add new information?

    These questions may be difficult for the novice researcher to answer, but comparing information in one source with that in another may provide some answers. For example, compare the coverage of "black holes" in *World Book Encyclopedia* with the article on the same topic in *McGraw-Hill Encyclopedia of Science and Technology*.

- Is the source too elementary, too technical, too advanced, or just right for your needs?

- What type of audience is the author addressing?

- Is the information aimed at a specialized or a general audience?

RELIABILITY

Objective or Biased Treatment
- Do the facts support the author's viewpoint?

(continued)

Table 1	EVALUATING INFORMATION SOURCES (continued)

RELIABILITY (continued)

Objective or Biased Treatment *(continued)*

• Do you detect individual biases in the writing?

• Does the author use language that is designed to appeal to emotions and prejudices?

• What is the author's motive in writing the work?

> Knowing something about the author's background, training, and other works is useful in determining possible bias. Often this information can be obtained from biographical dictionaries and indexes. The periodical indexes and abstracts might be checked to see if the author has written biased literature or if there has been controversy surrounding his or her publications.

• Is the information that is presented fact or opinion?

> It is not easy to separate fact from opinion. Facts can usually be verified; opinions, though they may be based on factual information, are based on the author's interpretation of facts. Skilled writers can manipulate their opinions so as to make you think their interpretations are facts. Note whether the work is well researched and documented.

• Is the work propaganda?

> Propaganda is easily recognized when it is in a leaflet that is handed out on the street corner, but can it be recognized in other media? Propaganda is material that is systematically distributed to advocate a point of view or a strongly held interest on an issue. Its purpose is to influence and change the opinions and behavior of others. Those who use propaganda tend to capitalize on events by playing on emotions and by exploiting human weaknesses and fears. However, all propaganda is not negative, especially when it is designed to accomplish good, such as a campaign to stop the use of drugs among teenagers or to combat neighborhood crimes. Politicians use propaganda when campaigning for public office; businesses use it to sell products. You need to be able to distinguish between good and bad propaganda.

Accuracy

• Is the information correct, or are there obvious errors in the information?

> It may be necessary to sample several sources to determine if there are inconsistencies in reporting such things as times, dates, and places. Statistical information is vulnerable to such inaccuracies, and one might do well to verify statistical information in more than one source whenever this is possible.

• Does the author cite the sources used?

• Does the author use primary or secondary sources?

Illustrations

• Does the work contain pictures, drawings, maps, or statistical tables that enhance its usefulness?

> The use of illustrations not only makes a book or article more interesting, but also makes a significant contribution to the understanding of the materials being presented.

(continued)

Table 1	EVALUATING INFORMATION SOURCES (continued)

CURRENCY

Date of Publication

- When was the work published?

- Is the information up-to-date or have discoveries been made or events taken place since the work was published?

  To determine currency of information, you might check journal articles on the same topic to see if there have been new events or developments. On Web pages, the date of the last revision is usually at the bottom of the home page, or sometimes on every page.

- Is the source current or too out-of-date for your topic?

  Current information is needed in areas that undergo constant and frequent changes such as in the pure and behavioral sciences. On the other hand, material that was written many years ago is often more suitable for topics in history and literature than those written more recently.

Table 2	EVALUATING INTERNET INFORMATION

AUTHORITATIVENESS

Author

- Is the author's name listed on the page?

  In many instances Web pages are created by Web masters whose expertise is more in page design than in familiarity with the content of the page. Also beware of anonymity.

- Is the author qualified to write on this subject?
- Are his or her education, training, and/or experience in a field relevant to the topic that is covered?

  Look on the page for biographical information, such as the author's title or position.

- Has the author published in other formats?
- Is there a way to contact the author? (E-mail or other address provided?)
- If the author is an organization, is it one that is well known and respected?

COMPREHENSIVENESS

- Is this a summary of a topic or does it cover all aspects of the topic?

  It is not unusual to find postings that are just excerpts or summaries of another work in a printed source.

- Are there links? Is there a brief description of the page?
- Does the site offer a selected list of resources in a particular discipline or field or does it claim to offer a complete list?
- If a selected list is offered, does the author explain how the list of resources was chosen?
- Does the site refer to print and other non-Internet resources or just Internet resources?

(continued)

Table 2 — EVALUATING INTERNET INFORMATION (continued)

RELIABILITY

- What is the origin of the site?

  Examine the site by checking the domain in the URL (Uniform Resource Locator) or Internet address. The domain name is the last part of the URL. The most common domains are "edu" for educational institutions, "gov" for government, "com" for commercial and "org" for organization. Countries outside of the United States use country codes as their domain names: for example, "ca" for Canada, and "fr" for France. Although government and education sites tend to be more reliable, information from commercial sites may also provide valid information. But keep in mind that commercial sites are probably more interested in selling you a product than in providing unbiased information.

- Does the site describe or provide the results of research or scholarly effort?
- Can the results be refuted or verified through other means—for example, in other research tools?
- Is advertising included on the site, and if so, does it affect the contents of the page?
- Does the page contain pictures, drawings, maps, or statistical tables that enhance its usefulness?
- Are there obvious signs of poor quality, such as bad grammar, colloquial speech, misspelled words, inflammatory words?
- Does the site contain propaganda?

  The Internet, as no other media in history, allows individuals from every walk of life and from throughout the world to put out messages that are designed to persuade and influence others to accept their point of view. You must be able to use your best judgment to distinguish propaganda from truly objective literature.

- Is this a *hoax*? Or an *urban legend*?

  A hoax is an attempt to trick others into believing that something that is a fake is real. Some hoaxes are humorous, intended as a practical joke. Others are mean spirited, designed to hurt or ridicule. Examples of hoaxes can be found at http://hoaxbusters.ciac.org/. *Urban legends* are stories that are not true but are presented as being factual. They are retold so many times that they have taken on an aura of truth. More information on urban legends can be found at: http://www.snopes.com/.

CURRENCY

- When was the information posted or updated?

  On Web pages, the date of the last revision is usually at the bottom of the home page, or sometimes on every page.

- What are the inclusive dates of the information?

EXERCISE 4. EVALUATING BOOKS AND JOURNAL ARTICLES IN PRINT

1. Locate a nonfiction book that interests you in the online catalog of your library or use a nonfiction book that you have read recently.

    Give the following information.

    a. Author of the book:

    b. Title:

    c. Publisher of the book:

    d. Publication date:

    e. Is this a primary or a secondary source?

    f. What is the level of scholarship? Popular or scholarly?

    g. Write a brief evaluation of the book based on the criteria listed in this chapter. For example, does the book include biographical information about the author? Is it sufficient to vouch for her or his authoritativeness? Explain.

2. Locate a journal in your library and give the following information.

   a. Title of the journal:

   b. Publisher of the journal:

   c. Date of the journal:

   d. Author of an article in the journal:

   e. Title of the article:

   f. Pages of the article:

   g. What is the level of scholarship? Popular or scholarly?

   h. Write a brief evaluation of the journal article based on the criteria listed in this chapter.

EXERCISE 5. HOAXES AND URBAN LEGENDS

1. Explore the health related hoaxes at the Center for Disease Control (http://www.cdc.gov/doc.do/id/ 0900f3ec80226b9c). Give the dates and titles of two of the hoaxes that are listed.

   a.

   b.

2. List the five top hoaxes from the Antivirus Resources: Virus or Hoax? site at http://virusall.com/ hoaxfive.shtml.

   a.

   b.

   c.

   d.

   e.

3. Select one of the hoaxes that interests you and summarize it.

4. Go to the Symantec virus hoax center at: http://www.symantec.com/avcenter/hoax.html and answer the following questions.

   a. What is a virus hoax?

   b. What action should you take if you receive an e-mail containing a virus warning?

5. Go to The Virus Information Library at: http://vil.mcafee.com/hoax.asp. Select two of the virus hoaxes listed on the page and give a brief description of each.

   a.

   b.

6. From the Hoaxbusters site (http://hoaxbusters.ciac.org/) select Hoax Categories.

   a. Under "Urban Myths," select "Voting Rights Expire." Write a brief summary of the hoax.

   b. Write a brief evaluation of the Hoaxbusters site. Use the criteria for reliability found in Table 1.

7. Go to the Urban Legends Reference Page (http://www.snopes.com/).
   Select the Politics category. Select "War/Anti-War" and answer the following questions.
   (Note: Review the explanation of codes before you find the urban legend.)

   a. How many of these legends are considered to be true?

   b. How many are considered false?

   c. On the Snopes.com homepage click on "site info" on the top of the page and answer the following questions.

      1) Who maintains the site?

      2) What is its purpose?

      3) How is it funded?

      4) Do you consider this a reliable site for information about hoaxes and urban legends? Explain your answer.

Chapter 5

Managing the Stresses of Life as a College Student

CASE STUDY

Nadir

Nadir and his wife have three boys between the ages of 6 and 12. Although he works full time, Nadir didn't think returning to college to get a degree would be too much for him. He signed up for two classes in the fall semester and plans to take three in the spring. However, it's near the end of the first semester, and he's already feeling the stress. He's highly motivated to succeed in college because he currently has a construction job and knows that he won't be able to do such a physically demanding job forever. His goal is to get into management or become a building inspector.

His job is somewhat seasonal, which gives him more time during the winter months to take classes, but the semester is not over when spring construction really picks up. Then the workload becomes intense. In addition, Nadir commutes to various job sites, which can add considerable time to his day. He would like to take more online or teleclasses, but most courses in his major are not offered in that format.

At home things are not all that stress-free either. Nadir's wife, Jennifer, and his recently widowed mother do not get along well. Some of their problems stem from cultural misunderstandings. He is an only son and feels a strong responsibility to take care of his mother. He knows that is what his father would have wanted him to do. His mother doesn't make it easy for him, though, as she expects Nadir to be at her beck-and-call every time she needs the least little thing done. She would never consider hiring strange workmen to come to her house. No; a good son should do whatever is needed.

All of the running around for his job and his mother doesn't leave Nadir much time for recreation, exercise, or to take care of the chores at his own house. He realizes he needs to spend quality time with Jennifer in order to keep their marriage strong. He would also like to spend more time with his boys. They need a father's influence and guidance, especially the preteen son.

The biggest stress of all is the approaching holiday season. Jennifer comes from a large family that has always made family gatherings the focal point of the holidays. A few years ago her parents divorced, and now her father is remarried. Celebrating with both of her parents adds to the already overcrowded schedule. At the same time, Nadir's mother expects them to spend the holidays with her, especially now that she is alone.

Nadir finds it difficult to concentrate on his studies and is struggling with his one-day-a-week algebra course. Not only is the class long, but the instructor covers several chapters at each session. Nadir is feeling quite anxious about the final exam. He needs to do well in order to build strong skills, pass the course with a "C" or better, and move on to the next math level.

Reflections

- What are some ways Nadir can spend time with his family while also taking care of his own needs?
- How might Nadir and Jennifer lessen the stress of the holiday season?
- What, if anything, can be done to help improve the relationship between Nadir's wife and mother?
- How can Nadir adjust his college schedule to accommodate all of the demands on his time?

INTRODUCTION

You probably didn't expect college to be easy, but many students are unprepared for how stressful going to college can be. As a college student, you are likely to have more roles than the average person. Most students work at least part time, but many are full-time employees. If you live at home, you probably have additional responsibilities. If you are married and/or a parent, you are aware of the time and energy involved in building strong relationships and running a household. If you're just starting to live on your own, you have the pressure of paying bills, grocery shopping, doing laundry, etc.—things that your parents used to do for you.

Many of you are also involved in activities either on campus or in the community. Now you've added the hours of homework and studying that it takes to maintain good grades. In addition, if you were not a strong student in high school, or if it has been a few years since you were in school, you might be feeling anxious about taking tests, working math problems, or writing papers. College courses move very quickly, and the pace frequently accelerates after midterm.

This chapter will help you *identify the things in your life that cause you stress*. In addition to college stressors, many people these days are trying to *deal with unreasonable feelings of anger*. Similar coping strategies are used in both anger and stress management. The *stress-reduction and relaxation techniques* introduced in this chapter may help you achieve balance in your life. *Math and test anxiety* are such common student stressors that a special section is devoted to ways of reducing them. So, if you're feeling a little stressed-out these days, read on; this chapter is for you.

Pretest

Identify the major changes that are happening in your life right now. Check as many as apply to you *within this past year.*

Family changes:

- Death of spouse, parent, sibling
- Death of grandparent or other close relative
- Divorce or marital separation (you or your parents)
- Marriage
- Pregnancy
- Gaining a new family member/s (birth, adoption, stepfamily, elder moving in, etc.)
- Major changes in health or behavior of a close family member

Health changes:

- Serious personal injury or illness
- Major change in sleeping habits
- Major change in eating habits
- Quitting, starting, or major increase in smoking, drinking, or other drug use
- Major change in amount of exercise or activities

Financial changes:

- Sudden loss of income
- Major change in financial status (a lot better or a lot worse-off than usual)
- Taking on a mortgage
- Foreclosure on a mortgage or loan
- Taking on a loan

Employment changes:

- Being fired
- Retiring
- Major change in work responsibilities (promotion, demotion, transfer)
- Changing careers
- Major change in working hours or conditions
- Major conflict with your boss/supervisor, or co-workers

Personal changes:

- Detention in jail or other institution
- Death of a close friend

- "Breaking-up" with girlfriend/boyfriend
- Conflict with spouse, in-laws, parents, or a close friend
- Beginning or ending formal education
- Moving to different residence/Major change in living conditions
- Outstanding personal achievement
- Revision of personal habits (dress, manners, associations, etc.)

Social changes:

- Changing to a new college
- Major change in usual type or amount of recreation
- Major change in church and/or social activities
- Vacation
- Major changes in holiday celebrations and/or number of family get-togethers

What does it mean? Change frequently causes stress. The more check marks—the more changes you have going on in your life—the higher your risk for a stress-related illness. If you have major changes taking place in all areas of your life (check marks in each category), that can also signal the potential for trouble.

WHAT IS STRESS?

Stress is the body's reaction to an occurrence or an event. You're driving to class and suddenly notice flashing lights and hear the siren of a police car behind you. Your body instinctively reacts. You look down at your speedometer; it shows 10 miles over the speed limit. Tension mounts. You prepare for what may follow. You don't really have time to stop and certainly can't afford a ticket. Your heart starts beating faster, and your mind is racing as you try to think of what to say. Even if the police car continues down the road, you may still feel a little shaken. Your adrenaline is high; you're stressed. A police car driving with its lights and siren turned on is not in itself a stressful event. If you were stopped at a red light on a side street or driving in the opposite direction, you would have a much different reaction to that event. The event is neutral, but your reaction to it can be positive or negative.

How we react in any situation is largely determined by our past experiences and our expectations of certain consequences or results. Our perceptions, beliefs, habits, level of self-confidence, and physical, mental, and emotional health also influence our reactions. No two people react exactly alike. What may be a challenge for one person may be distressful for another.

We usually think of stress as always being from negative or bad events, but stress also may occur from happy occasions. Starting college, planning a wedding, the birth of a child, celebrating the holidays with family, getting a new job, moving to a new house, or remodeling your current one are usually considered positive events. Yet, all of these can produce stress. *Change of any kind may produce stress.* That's why the pretest asked you to identify how many major changes are going on in your life right now. A little stress may be just what you need to motivate you. However, if you get too much stress in a very short time period, your body may become overloaded. When that happens, your natural immune system may be unable to defend itself against all of the germs, bacteria, and viruses that surround us. Your resistance is lowered, and you succumb to whatever illness is "going around." Being overloaded for a long period of time can be very damaging to your health. That's why it is important for you to use common sense and practice good health habits as your first line of defense.

Stress is unavoidable and affects everyone. Relationships with our families, friends, and others, as well as money, health, work, and college issues may all produce stress. Anger is a normal emotion that, if left unchecked, can result in serious problems. Major life events, everyday irritations, conflicts, and frustrations frequently result in feelings of anger that also boost our heart rate, adrenaline, and blood pressure levels. A specific event, such as a traffic delay that causes you to be late for class or work, or a specific person, e.g., a co-worker who is frequently late thus causing you to work overtime, both result in angry feelings that you need to resolve to eliminate further stress.

Sometimes we "set ourselves up" by developing unrealistic goals or setting our standards too high. When we expect too much of ourselves by overrating our abilities, we may fail to make satisfactory progress toward or not achieve our goals. Failure can produce a state of depression that prevents us from functioning effectively. The opposite is also true. We may set our standards too low or not try to achieve. Then, we're stressed by the consequences of our laziness and irresponsibility.

Another cause of stress is a conflict in our values. When we are in situations where we act contrary to our core beliefs and values, we feel the pressure of being phony. Time constraints or the feeling of always being overloaded is yet another huge stressor. When we lack the proper support and/or resources or feel that college or job demands interfere with our personal activities, we may exhaust our abilities to reduce or resist stress.

HOW TO REDUCE STRESS AND MANAGE YOUR ANGER

We cannot control all of life's stressors, but we can control our reactions to the people and events that cause us to become angry or stressed. Identify what is causing your stress, and then implement your own personal stress-reduction program. If you alter your beliefs and your way of thinking, you can reduce anxiety levels and their negative effects on your body. Stress is manageable, providing it does not approach a life-threatening level.

Step One: Look for Stress Symptoms—Be aware of the symptoms of anger and stress. Awareness always precedes action. Recognize the symptoms and don't deny that you have them. Be especially aware of times when you may "lose control" by using loud/abusive language, criticizing others, withdrawing socially, or inappropriately confronting others. You can start to solve the problem once you know it exists.

Step Two: Identify Stressful Times, Situations, and People—Identify the times and places when stress strikes you. Did you respond strongly to any of the pretest items? Think of the current causes of stress or anger "triggers" in your life right now. If it helps, keep a diary to pinpoint problem issues. Record what happened and your reaction. Think of other possible ways you could have reacted. List the kinds of things that were helpful in relieving the stress or reducing your anger level.

Step Three: Eliminate Unnecessary Stress—Whenever possible, eliminate the causes of unnecessary stress. From your diary you might have noticed a pattern of things or people that always stress you. When you come to that situation/person again, try to change your response. Don't jump to conclusions, and refuse to let anger and frustrations take over. Then, avoid those stressful situations. "That's easier said than done," you say, but remember that you control your own actions and reactions.

Changing your physical environment or your timing may also help you reduce your stress.

- Plan a different route if traffic jams cause you to become tense or you tend to develop "road rage."
- Shop at "off-peak" hours if you hate waiting in line at the grocery or mall.
- Try to schedule discussions on important issues with family members, friends, or co-workers when you feel alert and refreshed rather than just reacting without thought.
- If possible, take ten minutes for "personal down-time" to be alone when you arrive home from work, and let the stress of the day fade away.
- Be sure to take a few minutes for yourself during your workday.

You cannot change someone else, but you can change yourself and your attitudes. Don't let conflict with your significant others become your way of life. It's too exhausting and frustrating. Learn new skills such as assertive communication to improve and soften all your relationships.

Step Four: Reduce the Effects of Unavoidable Stress—For the stress in your life that you can't eliminate, try to control and reduce its effects. Remember to keep your perspective. Think about how important this event really is. Will you even remember it next week? Next month? If not, why get upset about it? Keep your stress at a minimum, and don't overreact.

It may not be possible to reduce all of life's irritations. Keep in mind that reacting with anger is ultimately a choice. Angry responses such as yelling, hitting, or confronting others can be outright aggressive. They may also be passive-aggressive—for example, backstabbing, gossiping, or manipulating others.

People have successfully dealt with the stress in their lives by using some of the techniques listed in Table 1.

Relaxation and Anger Management Techniques

It is difficult to eliminate all the stress in your life, but you can learn to reduce your anger and control your frustrations or anxiety by practicing relaxation exercises. Some are more involved, but others are simple enough to do anywhere—even in the classroom. Try one or more of the following exercises whenever you feel yourself becoming angry, tense, or overly tired, or if you feel that others may be taking advantage of you.

Deep Breathing

Anger and stress result in shallow, rapid breathing. Deep, slow breathing can reduce stress and help you relax. Oxygen is the body's natural stress-reducer, and increasing your body's oxygen intake helps relieve tension. Begin by closing your eyes. Exhale slowly, and clear the

Table 1   COMMON STRESS REDUCERS

ESTABLISH SUPPORT SYSTEMS	MANAGE YOUR TIME
• Keep the positive, supportive relationships you have and build new ones. • Ask for help when you need it. • Use available campus and community resources.	• Develop a schedule using "Time Management" techniques. • Simplify your life. • Learn to say "No" to requests that are not priorities. • Delegate when necessary. • Use mini "downtime" breaks.

PRACTICE EMOTIONAL CONTROL	MAINTAIN A HEALTHY LIFESTYLE
• Use assertive communication techniques to prevent anger/frustration from causing undue stress. • Eliminate self-defeating behaviors and keep things in perspective. • Practice forgiveness. • Use cooperation rather than confrontation to reach your goals. • Be willing to compromise and seek alternative solutions to problems. • Use humor and laughter to lighten your emotional load. • Seek professional counseling if necessary.	• Eat nutritionally-balanced meals. • Get plenty of sleep. • Exercise regularly. • Avoid using drugs, including alcohol and tobacco. • If sexually active, protect yourself and your partner from sexually transmitted diseases or from unwanted pregnancy. • Take time for yourself—do whatever you enjoy to help promote balance in your life. • Try massage therapy or other relaxation techniques.

UNDERSTAND YOURSELF	ACCEPT CHANGE AND LEARN NEW SKILLS
• Think through what you really believe and why you believe it. • Be open to new experiences and ideas. • Practice critical thinking when faced with decisions. • Use your faith for motivation and to guide you through difficult situations.	• Learn something new to energize and revitalize your spirit and to increase your productivity. • Accept change with a positive attitude and as an opportunity to grow.

air from your lungs. Then inhale deeply through your nose and hold your breath for a count of five. When taking a deep breath, your stomach (actually, your diaphragm) should be expanded. Slowly exhale, using your lips to control the rate of air that you move out of your lungs. Begin the cycle again. Repeat several times until you feel calmer. You can do this anywhere and any time you feel stressed, whether you are taking an exam or confronting a family member or co-worker.

Deep Muscle Relaxation

One of the most common reactions to anger and stress is muscle tension. Think of a time when you've been very angry or frustrated, and remember the tenseness in your jaw, neck, shoulders, arms, and hands. Deep and progressive muscle relaxation will help you relax your entire body from head to toe by first tensing and then relaxing the various muscle groups. The whole process can take anywhere from one to twenty minutes.

Find a comfortable position either sitting or lying down. If you are alone, you may want to loosen any tight clothing. Close your eyes. Begin with your head and facial muscles—scalp, brow, eyes, lips, jaw, etc. Tighten your muscles and hold tense for ten seconds, then relax. Continue contracting and relaxing your muscles by moving through your neck, shoulder, back, and chest areas. Keep doing this through every major muscle group. Concentrate on your breathing (slow, deep breaths) while you work your way down to your hips, legs, and feet.

When you have completed all the muscle groups, you will feel refreshed, calm, and relaxed. This type of relaxation may also help you sleep better. You can do a shortened version of this exercise in class or almost anywhere. Close your eyes; tense up all of your muscles for a couple of seconds; then release them slowly, one body part at a time.

Meditation

An ancient relaxation technique—meditation—can help you clear stressful thoughts from your mind, but it may take time to learn how to do it effectively. Find a location where you are comfortable and won't be disturbed. Close your eyes and focus on a peaceful word or image. Your goal is to find a quiet, peaceful state of mind. Concentrate on something calming, and do not let any other thoughts enter your mind. Learning to abandon all other thoughts is the hard part. Return to the one image or word you have selected, clearing your mind of any stress and worry. Breathe deeply. At the end of your meditation session, you will feel calm and relaxed.

Imagery

Imagery is another type of mental exercise. It is like taking a mini, mental vacation or daydreaming with a purpose. You can achieve the same feeling of tranquility that you do with meditation, but the technique is different. Rather than concentrating on a single thought, you create an entirely relaxing, though imaginary, place of your own to which you can escape. Once again, close your eyes and visualize the perfect place to relax. It might be in the woods by a brook, on a warm, sandy beach, in the mountains, floating on a cloud—wherever seems right to you. See yourself there, calm and satisfied with life. You can go to this special place in your mind whenever you need a few seconds of escape-time. You can also use this technique to build confidence. While in your perfect place, visualize yourself accomplishing one of your goals.

Pampering Yourself

There are a variety of products currently on the market to help you relax. Everything from bubble bath to scented candles can be used to create a soothing environment. Relaxing music, pleasant aromas, multimedia that captures the sights and sounds of ocean waves, raindrops, a crackling fire, or any number of other auditory and visual images can produce a tranquil state of mind. Massage therapy is now readily available in a variety of forms—chair massages for the neck and shoulders, pulse or wave massages, and full-body massages.

STUDENT STRESSORS

Adjusting to new and unfamiliar situations is a cause of stress for most people, and students are no exception. A new college, new course, or new instructor may create a great deal of anxiety. How much depends on his/her personality and past experiences. For a student, quizzes, tests, and final examinations can induce stress. A more extreme form is called test anxiety. Another high stressor for students is their fear of math. Both of these kinds of anxiety could be caused by a history of not doing well in school or on tests, having poor study skills, fear of failure, and outside pressures.

Test Anxiety

It is not abnormal to be anxious about a test. Almost everyone feels some apprehension, fear, uneasiness, or worry about taking a test. A little pressure can be beneficial if it is moderate and controlled, and some students view an exam as an opportunity to show what they can do. Their attitude is similar to that of an athlete who enjoys competition because it enhances his/her own performance. If moderate anxiety keeps you alert and provides you with a burst of energy, it can help you do your best.

Test anxiety may result in noticeable physical symptoms such as headaches, nausea, sweating, or dizziness. It can reduce your ability to concentrate and make you feel overwhelmed and unable to perform. The anxiety is self-induced, but outside pressures to maintain good grades may be contributing factors. If you suffer from anxiety because you think you have to be perfect, you need to let go of some of your unrealistic expectations. When stress and anxiety become so extreme that they affect your performance or become detrimental and threatening to your well-being, however, you may need the help of a professional to get your anxiety under control. If your anxiety is less extreme, you may be able to use the following strategies to handle it yourself.

Test Anxiety Reduction

- **Attitude Adjustment**—Be realistic about the importance of any single test or exam. What is the worst that could happen? You could get a lower grade than you wished; you could be embarrassed about your performance; you could fail the test; or a poor test grade could cause you to fail a course in which you are struggling. You might even lose an opportunity for a scholarship or have to pay back some of your financial aid. Yes; these are all terrible consequences, but none of them will determine the outcome of the rest of your life. A test is just a test—usually part of your total grade for one course in any one semester. Recognize that your value as a person is not dependent on what you do on any one test or in any one course.

- **Effective Study Techniques**—Previous chapters have introduced you to strategies and techniques designed to increase your ability to perform successfully in the classroom. Faithfully practicing the note-taking, time management, and test-taking strategies outlined in this book will give you the confidence you need to go into the test with a winning attitude. Be sure to use tutoring and other academic support services as needed.

- **Positive Self-Talk**—Negative thinking increases your anxiety levels. Recognize any self-defeating thoughts you might have and replace them with positive thoughts designed to increase your confidence levels. Believe that you have the ability to control what happens and visualize yourself doing your absolute best. Practice using positive statements to boost your confidence and self-esteem. In your mind, tell yourself, "I am well prepared; I am confident; I will do my best."

Math Anxiety

The physical and psychological reactions to math that affects performance in class and keeps you from remembering what you learned when taking a math test is termed math anxiety. It is usually the result of negative past experiences. Most students with math anxiety can trace its roots to a school experience that convinced them they could not be successful in mathematics. Sometimes the pressure to do well, or conversely, the excuse to do poorly, came from parents and/or other family members.

If you suffer from math anxiety, think about your first negative experience with math. Was it failing to learn the multiplication tables right away? Was it being made to stand at the board in front of the class until you could work out a difficult problem? Was it the result of someone telling you, "You'll never be good in math"? To combat the causes of math anxiety, you need to recognize their sources, reject the untrue things you've been programmed to believe, and adopt a new approach—a willingness to go at it with a fresh start. If math anxiety can be learned (and it is), then it can be unlearned.

Math Anxiety Reduction

Effectively reducing math anxiety requires most students to combat negative self-images about their ability to be successful in math by taking positive steps to change their attitudes. First, they must develop and practice strong math study skills. Each small success in math performance will build confidence levels.

How can you change a negative attitude about math? Start by examining the math myths listed in Table 2, and become aware that these common assumptions are, indeed, myths.

Table 2   FALSE ASSUMPTIONS ABOUT MATH

- Math is linear and logical; therefore, creative people cannot be good in math.
- There is only one right way to solve a math problem.
- Women are not good in math. It's genetic. Variation: No one in my family is good in math; therefore, I can't/won't be good in math.
- Math has no value in the real world.
- I haven't been good at math in the past, and it's too late for me to learn math now.
- Math is hard and boring.
- It doesn't help to ask questions because I won't understand the explanation anyway.
- I've always been good in English, so I can't expect to be good in math.
- Math isn't logical.

Now that you've recognized these math myths, take a look at the following **math facts**:

- Math is sequential, building upon itself, so it is important to study every day. Studying once a week will not produce the same results as keeping up daily, especially if you have a class that meets three or more times per week.
- The key to solving math problems is practice. Keep up with your homework and work the problems whether or not the instructor collects or grades homework.
- It is more important to understand the concepts, principles, and relationships than it is to memorize the formulas and work the problems.
- Choosing math courses that meet as many times a week as possible is to your advantage. Classes that meet only once or twice a week tend to produce stress, especially for students who do not excel at math. If you don't understand the material, you may have to wait a whole week to ask your questions. In a five-day-per-week course, fewer concepts can be presented per day, which gives you time to practice before moving to the next topic.
- Avoid taking math during accelerated summer sessions because these sessions are even more intense and move *much more rapidly* than the traditional fall/spring semester courses.
- Missing a math class can cause a real gap in your knowledge and understanding. Remember, math is sequential. Missing any material can cause confusion and lack of understanding.
- Math anxiety is learned, and it can be unlearned.

We've reviewed some common myths and some truths about math. If you have difficulties with math and/or math anxiety, how can you counteract any negative attitudes you may have developed? First, you need to examine your past math experiences. Can you remember the first time you felt unhappy with your math performance? If you can uncover the source of your negative attitude, you can work on changing it to a positive one. If your problems with math stem from knowledge gaps or not understanding some fundamental concepts, then you can correct them by working in a computerized learning center or taking a basic math course to learn what you don't know.

Take a look at your current attitude. Do you truly believe that you will never be successful at math, or are you willing to change your attitude? The following tips for improving math performance will help you build a stronger, more positive attitude.

- Confront any math myths you've held in the past and recognize that they are myths.
- Use the relaxation techniques and positive self-talk approaches discussed earlier in the chapter to help you develop a positive attitude about your math ability.
- Attend every math class, take good notes, and record all steps in the examples covered in class so you will remember them later.
- Ask questions in class and seek tutorial assistance as soon as you do not understand any material. *Don't get behind!* Remember that sequential process.
- Review as soon as possible after class.
- Before registering for your next math class, talk to other students and try to identify instructors who are receptive to questions, use cooperative learning techniques, review material prior to tests, and teach in a style that matches your learning style.

Do all of your assignments and the sample problems provided. Practice makes perfect.

Practice the following steps to help you solve math problems:

- Make sure you understand basic definitions, symbols, and other math terminology.
- Know and understand the formula being used.
- Read the problem aloud.
- Draw a picture to help you see relationships within the problem.
- Examine the problem. Ask,
  □ What information is given?
  □ Specifically, what do I need to find?
  □ What do I need to do?
- Estimate the end result.
- Ask yourself if your answer makes common sense.
- Check your answer.
- Practice until you understand how to do that kind of problem perfectly and completely.

SUMMARY

We all live complicated lives and are faced with stress on a daily basis. Moderate amounts of stress are normal and sometimes can motivate us to do our best. Too much stress, however, can cause serious physical, emotional, and behavioral problems.

Math and test anxieties are common problems experienced by many students. Both are learned responses that can be unlearned. Practicing good study habits, having a realistic attitude about the importance of tests in our lives, practicing positive self-talk, using relaxation techniques, and dispelling the math myths we have been taught will help us create success experiences.

We need to acquire the skills necessary to control or eliminate excessive stress in our lives. A number of strategies to help you develop your own stress management program were covered in this chapter. Maintaining a healthy lifestyle, using support systems, and practicing relaxation techniques are especially effective. If you have very high stress levels that have lasted for long periods of time, seek professional help. Remember that you can reduce many of your life stressors by identifying the people and events that cause you stress. Change the things in your life over which you have control, and release the rest. Don't worry; be happy!

JOURNAL QUESTIONS

In the case study, Nadir faced many stressors. Which of the suggestions in this chapter would help him deal more effectively with them?

Now think about your own life and continue your essay by writing a response to one or both of the topics below.

1. Do you have test or math anxiety (or both)? To what do you attribute your fear of taking tests and/or your problems with math? What do you need to do to overcome these fears? List several strategies you will use.

2. Identify the major causes of stress in your life. Describe how you can eliminate some of them and what strategies you will use to reduce the effects of stress that can't be eliminated.

EXERCISE 1. ACADEMIC ANXIETY

When taking math or other difficult courses, how much effort do you make to ensure that you can be successful?

Check your responses to the following:

	Usually do	Sometimes do	Never thought about it
Course Selection I schedule my difficult classes at a time when I am most alert. I choose instructors that match my learning style. I schedule the next course in a sequence as soon as I complete the prerequisite course.			
Preparing for and Taking Tests I keep up-to-date so I don't have to cram the night before the test. I look over the entire test before I begin. If necessary, I take the full amount of time allotted. I carefully review and check my answers before I turn in the test. When my tests are returned, I keep track of the kinds of mistakes I've made. If I don't understand what I did wrong, I meet with the instructor after class or during her/his office hours to make certain I will be able to work a similar problem correctly (e.g., on the final exam).			
General Anxiety Issues I believe that I can be academically successful. I recognize that preparedness will help lessen any anxiety. I know and am willing to practice simple relaxation techniques.			

Look at your responses in the "sometimes do" or "never thought about it" column. Outline the steps you can take so your responses will be "usually do" for your next test or when you next register for classes.

_____

_____

_____

_____

_____

Chapter 6

The Art of Test Taking

INTRODUCTION

Testing is the age old method of finding out what students know about assigned course information and/or how well they have mastered a skill. Examinations force students into learning material and provide the instructor with feedback on how well they have been taught a subject and whether they need to modify their delivery of course information. Test results also provide students with information on how well they are progressing in the course. This information should tell students if they need to modify their method of studying in order to successfully pass the course.

Since testing is such an important college survival skill, you need to know just how it is done and what the rules are for succeeding. Therefore, this chapter will provide tips and strategies on how to effectively prepare for and take tests. It will also emphasize the importance of preparing for tests.

Taking tests is a four part process that requires a lot of work on the part of the student. Testing is a skill. Therefore, it must be practiced in order to learn it. You have to work at being a successful test taker just as you must practice and rehearse any other skill you want to learn. The four part process consists of the following:

- General Preparation
- Test Specific Preparation
- Taking the Test
- Reviewing After the Test

You must be a smart student if you want to pass the test. The smart student is sufficiently motivated and understands why he or she must pass the test. Remember, it is not always the most intelligent, organized, or the best students who do well on a test and earn good grades. It is those students who have developed good study skills in test preparation and are committed to passing a course. These are generally the students who perform well at exam time. They are committed, time conscious and, once again, organized and are willing to put in a sufficient amount of time in test preparation to make the grade. Here are some **tips** to help you understand this process.

GENERAL PREPARATION—PART I

Tip 1: Know the planning rules for effective studying.

Start studying for exams from the first day of class. When talking with the instructor after you have received the course syllabus, be sure to ask the following questions:

a. What are the major goals of the course?

b. What kinds of exams do you normally give? Do you have any copies of some of your old exams I may use to help me prepare for your exams?

c. How many units or chapters are usually covered on an exam if it is not already in the syllabus?

d. Does the instructor expect you to remember general or specific detail, deduction, and/or opinions?

e. Will the tests normally cover class texts, lecture and other assigned materials such as films, periodicals, etc.?

f. Will make-up exams be allowed if I fail or miss a test?

g. How much will each exam count toward passing the course?

Tip 2: Develop a systematic method of studying.

If you do not develop this system, it will be difficult for you to be a successful test taker. Use the following rules to develop your system.

a. Learn the vocabulary of the course. Many students fail because they do not understand the vocabulary on exams.

b. Establish a study group or find a study partner from the class. Never go through a class without connecting with at least one other person in that class. You will have a built-in system for getting class notes you missed or for cross-checking information. In a study group, each person is responsible for units of information which they must share/teach to others in the group. This is good because when you have to teach information to someone else, you are more likely to learn it.

c. Always scan your chapter before you read. Then read the introduction and summary. These two parts of the chapter should help you to zero in on what you need to know. Do not read your textbooks as if you are reading a suspense or romance novel. Read with the knowledge or understanding of what is on the next page. Make connections.

d. Always read with a question and/or objective in mind. Never read aimlessly. Take the information in like your exam is tomorrow. Know the objectives your instructor wants you to cover. For each unit covered, ask the instructor to share the *must know* items.

e. Always do a quick review before going to class.

f. Take good notes from lecture and/or assigned readings.

g. Immediately after each lecture/reading assignment, organize your information the way it should be remembered. Rewrite your notes if necessary. Preferably a rewrite should be done within 24 hours of the class/review.

h.   Once material is organized, master it before you go back to class and take in new information. **Mapping** is a method that can help you organize material. See the example "Kinds of Examinations" in Table 1. Why don't you try making one for all of your courses.

i.   It is a good practice to take weekly tests on new information. This will help in moving information from short-term to long-term memory.

j.   This is the time to develop mnemonics if necessary.

k.   Use flash cards. You may use these cards to review or test. You can take them places where you are not allowed to take books or tablets. A flash card is a 3" x 5" card with the question on one side and the answer on the opposite side.

TEST SPECIFIC PREPARATION—PART II

Tip 3: Know how to "Get Ready."

a.   Ask the instructor for the format of the test. Format refers to kinds of test such as **objective**—true/false, multiple choice, matching, fill in the blanks—and **subjective**—essay and short answer. Objective exams require precise information. Subjective exams usually are not as precise, but require you to support the data. The test formats are discussed later in this chapter. **Remember**, smart students test themselves before the instructor tests them. In preparing for an exam, they develop a test similar to what they think the instructor will give in class and take it under what they perceive as the same classroom testing conditions. Test preparation can be demanding but its the smart thing to do.

b.   Ask the instructor what areas/chapters the test will cover. If you ask, some instructors will even tell you what questions will be on the test. Make sure you have all information from which the test questions will be taken.

c.   Study with a classmate whom you know does well in the course. It makes no sense to study with someone who is failing and cannot help you.

d.   Establish the test date and how much time you will have to complete the test when it is given.

e.   Set up a time schedule of pre-exam activities based on the date of the exam and your other life tasks (cooking, housekeeping, working, sharing). In preparing for the exam, you may have to sacrifice social, domestic, and some sleeping time.

f.   Develop test questions from lecture notes and assigned work.

g.   Equally divide your objectives and/or anticipated test questions so that you learn and review a certain portion each day. Remember to consider the complexity of each question/objective. Learning a portion each day or over a period of time is called spaced learning. **Do not cram.** If you have not done so already, turn all objectives for the units or areas to be covered on the exam into questions. Write out your answers for all of them. If you are studying for a skill class such as mathematics, practice the processes until you are able to work them without guessing and/or repeatedly looking at your notes. You need to be able to clearly distinguish formulas and/or rules. **SKILL CLASSES REQUIRE A LOT OF PRACTICE.**

h.   When you sit down to study, always review all information previously studied before moving on to new study questions.

Nicole is enrolled in Psychology and Professor Cooper has just announced a test for next Friday. He has given them thirty items to study and has indicated that the test will be a combination of objective and essay questions. Nicole works 12–16 hours a day on weekends. The only time she has for studying is during the week. So today she needs to make sure she has all of the notes and information from which the test will be drawn. Based on the test information, she has 4 days to prepare. She must also begin to determine which items may be asked objectively or in essay form.

Mon. 10 items	Tues. 10 items	Wed. 10 items	Thurs. Test/Rev	Fri. Test Day

Day One   Master the 1st 10 items/test yourself

Day Two   Review the 1st 10 items
           Master the 2nd 10 items/test yourself

Day Three Review the 1st 20 items
           Master the 3rd 10 items/test yourself

Day Four   Retest yourself on all items/review

Day Five   Arrive early enough to relax/then take test

Note: You should use a realistic time table that takes into consideration your daily responsibilities and the difficulty of the material to be learned.

---

i.   Ideally, the day before exams should be for briefly reviewing materials and not trying to take in new data. Get a good night's rest and get to class early so you can have time to relax before the exam. **Do not** use this time to cram in new information. **Knowing the testable information is one of the greatest deterrents to test anxiety. Knowing the information really inspires confidence.**

Tip 4: Know how to "Get Set."

a.   Anticipate test questions and their format if you don't already have them.

b.   Design a test on how you think the instructor is going to test you. Now test yourself with your notes and book closed just as they do in most class settings. Try to approximate the classroom environment. Set a timer or have someone call you when the time is up.

c.   Grade your test through the eyes of your instructor. Review again if necessary.

TAKING THE TEST—PART III

Tip 5: Know how to "Go." You are in the classroom and have the test in your hand. You are now going to take the test.

    a.   Read the directions. Make sure you understand them. Now is the time to ask for clarifications. Do not argue with the tester.

    b.   Scan the entire test before you begin.

    c.   Dump data as quickly as possible by lightly writing it on the back of your test or wherever it's feasible. This data refers to information that you are still holding in short term memory or that you have had difficulty retaining. **This may include acrostics and acronyms.**

    d.   Pay attention to qualifiers and absolute words.

    e.   Underline key words in directions and questions.

    f.   Now take a deep breath.

    g.   Develop a time strategy based on the number or questions and their point value.

    h.   Focus on your exam and do not let the behavior of other students distract you. For instance, some students panic when they see other students passing their papers in before them or busily writing when they are not.

    i.   If you are asked to do an essay, develop a brief outline first beginning with the main points.

    j.   When completing objective questions and you are using a scantron answer card, be sure to line up the questions and answers.

    k.   Read questions carefully and answer the easy ones first.

    l.   When reading questions, watch for grammatical agreements. This may help you in answering some of the items.

    m.   Look for answers in other questions.

    n.   Look for clue words.

    o.   Use the guessing or "bulling" rule if you don't know the answer. Bulling refers to coming as close as you possibly can with your answer. Be creative. Try to respond to all questions whether objective or essay. The only time you should leave a question unanswered is when there is a penalty and you are definitely unsure.

    p.   Make time to look over your test before passing it in to the instructor.

REVIEW AFTER THE EXAM—PART IV

Tip 6: Take a deep breath, review and modify if necessary.

    a.   Reward and praise yourself if you did well on the test.

    b.   Review answers to all questions you did not know and/or had to guess on before coming to the next class.

    c.   Analyze what you did right and what behaviors *you must modify* before the next test.

d. If you believe you did everything right and still did not pass the test, visit your instructor and let him or her give you analysis of the test items. It will help you to focus on weak areas.

e. Immediately put into practice your new behaviors.

Table 1	KINDS OF EXAMINATIONS
TYPE	RULES
Multiple-choice	1. Consist of stems, choices, distracters. 2. Read the entire stem and choices. 3. Eliminate the distracters. 4. Select your answer from the remaining choices. 5. When more than one choice is correct, look for the choice "all of the above," or certain other designations. 6. When more than one choice is incorrect, look for the choice indicating some of the choices or none of the choices. 7. It saves times to answer the easy ones first. 8. There are few situations in which something is always or never true.
True/False	1. True/false tests are not the easiest. Don't be fooled. 2. Make sure you understand what is being asked. 3. You always have a 50-50 chance of getting the item correct. 4. For a true/false statement to be true, the entire statement must be true. 5. Conversely, if any part of the statement is false, the statement is false. 6. Beware of absolute words such as all, none, every, and always. 7. Statements containing qualifiers such as some, sometimes, most, or often are frequently true.
Completion	1. You must know the correct information. 2. Sometimes clues are placed in the question. 3. Pay attention to words that precede the blank(s). 4. The grammatical structure of the sentence can help in determining what the instructor is looking for in an answer.
Matching	1. It is critical that you pay attention to directions. 2. Sometimes within the directions you will find that an answer may be used twice or only once. 3. If an item has only one correct answer, look for the more correct or complete answer. 4. As you collect responses (answers) cross them out so you don't waste time re-reading them again.

Table 1	KINDS OF EXAMINATIONS (continued)
TYPE	**RULES**
Essay	1. Outline what you plan to cover. 2. Present your information in a clear, concise, neat, and organized manner. This includes writing legibly. 3. Deal with the aspects of the topic the instructor has requested. 4. Pay attention to Key words since they tend to tell you how you are to deal with the topic. 5. Remember that most essay questions measure your depth of the knowledge of the subject and expect you to integrate and apply that knowledge. 6. State main points and use examples to support them. 7. Please refrain from excessive verbiage. Long answers do not equate to good grades.

Key Words

Discuss or explain	Examine in detail. Give facts, reasons, pros, cons.
Compare	Explain similarities and differences.
Contrast	Only explain the differences.
Critique/Evaluate	Give your opinion on the good and bad aspects of the facts as presented.
Describe	Present a mental picture consisting of the characteristics and/or how something really is.
Define	Give the meaning (not your opinion).
Enumerate	State points and briefly explain one by one.
Illustrate	Use examples to explain.
Interpret	Use your own words to explain.
Identify	Be specific in listing/naming items in a category.
Outline	Describe the major facts/ideas that are relevant to a subject.
Prove/Justify	Use evidence or logic based on facts to support an argument/idea.
Relate	Show the connection between ideas and points.
Summarize	Present the main ideas usually in paragraph form.
Trace	Describe the progress or development of an event.

Practice Test

Practicec your test-taking skills by taking the following timed quiz. Please follow directions. Before you begin, read all the items carefully. Each question is worth ten points.

1. Write your name here. _____

2. Identify one concept that you know you have learned well in this course.

   _____

   _____

3. Briefly explain it. _____

   _____

   _____

4. When you compare and contrast, you are

   _____

5. In a true/false question, there is always a   percent chance that the item is true.

6. Multiple choice questions consist of the   ,

                          and   ,

7. In true/false items, in order for it to be   the entire statement must be true.

8. In true/false questions, be aware of   .

9. Once you receive your test in hand, the first rule is to   .

10. Add the date beside your name in item number one and do not complete the other nine items.

How did you do? Question number one should be the only one answered with your name and today's date. The rest of the blanks should be empty. Subtract ten points for every one you attempted to answer.

TEST ANXIETY

"I really studied for this test but when I got in there, I couldn't remember a thing." "When I looked at the first question and couldn't answer it, I knew I was a goner." "I'm always afraid of exams because I never do well." "I'm so nervous, my hands sweat. I can't think and when I look around, everybody is working away but me."

Most of you have probably heard some of these statements before. They reflect how these persons are responding to test anxiety. Test anxiety is stress related to testing. Stress is defined as "the body's response to any demand made on it." The demand in this case is a combination of the test preparation and the test itself. On the one hand, you need to know that a little anxiety is good for everybody. It keeps us alert and on our toes. It keeps us from being too relaxed. If we are too relaxed, sometimes we take things for granted and don't prepare as we should. On the other hand, too much worry/anxiety keeps us from performing as we should. When one's anxiety level is very high, we know that it interferes with your memory and as a result drives information from your mind that you know you are more than familiar with.

Anger, depression, and a lack of confidence are other emotions that can also block memory. According to Atkinson and Longman, "test anxiety is a cycle in which self-doubt—even by a well-prepared student—causes the panic that results in a poor grade. The poor grade reinforces the feelings of self-doubt, which causes more panic and again self failure." When grades are tied to fear of loss and expectations of others, the anxiety level increases and once again causes one not to perform as is desired. Another factor to be considered is one's inability to concentrate on test preparation and the test once it is placed in your hands. You are not able to control your thoughts. Having counseled many students, I have found that the number one problem is really a lack of adequate preparation for the test. Most students simply are not test smart. An example of this would be the student who never tested himself/herself prior to the test under similar conditions as the instructor would do—closed book and timed. How do you respond to anxiety? Do you know the causes?

In the following exercises, think about what happens to you when you are anxious and what you think are the causes. For instance, a symptom might be a migraine headache. Working in a small group, complete the exercise on your own paper and then share information. Once you have made your list of symptoms and causes, discuss ways to overcome them. See exercise 3.

If you know that you have prepared well for the exam and you are failing, you may need to make an appointment with your school counselor. If you are one of those students who get ill at the thought of a test or upon walking into the test room, run to a professional counselor. You need help. If the reason you worry is because you have not studied, began to do so now and eliminate your anxiety. Refer to the information on how to prepare for tests. However, the basic rule to rid oneself from normal test anxiety, is to learn to relax. Professionals try to teach you how to desensitize yourself to anxiety through a form of relaxation. The theory is that you cannot be tense and relaxed at the same time. Hence, if you know the information and you can get rid of thoughts that are blocking your memory and causing panic, you can get back control of your thoughts and memory. It sounds simple, right?

During preparation and the exam itself, use deep breathing and muscle relaxing techniques to calm yourself. Close your eyes momentarily and breathe in and out focusing on something other than the exam. Focus by imagining a relaxing scene or situation. If that does not work, tense and relax your muscles while sitting in the chair with your feet flat on the floor and with your hands holding on to the sides of the chair. Tense and let go. Tense and let go. Do this four to five times while breathing in and out. To relax your hands, make tight fists and slowly release them. Do this a few times. In exercise 3, using your own paper, preferably the same one you used in Exercise 2, tell us some of the things you do to calm your anxiety level.

SUMMARY

This chapter has covered the reasons instructors give tests, the four parts of the test taking process and offered ideas on why we have test anxiety and how to cope with it.

Instructors give tests to assist the student in: mastering skills, learning course information, understanding how well they are progressing and whether they need to modify their method of studying for the course. Instructors also give tests to gauge how well they are teaching and getting the information over to students and whether they need to modify their method of delivery.

The four parts of the test taking process consist of: (1) *general preparation,* (2) *test specific preparation,* (3) *taking the test, and* (4) *reviewing immediately after the test.*

Test anxiety is stress related to testing, and this feeling is caused by physical and mental symptoms. Some are lack of confidence, inability to concentrate, fear of failure and the expectation of others. Being prepared for tests along with breathing and muscle relaxation exercises are some of the ways to cope with test anxiety.

REFERENCES

Atkinson, Rhonda Holt and Longman, Debbie G. *Getting Oriented.* West Publishing Company: New York, 1995.

Blerkom, Diana L. *College Study Skills: Becoming a Strategic Learner.* Wadsworth Publishing Company: Belmont, CA, 1994.

Cirlin, Alan. *Simple Rules for Success in College.* Kendall/Hunt Publishing Company: Dubuque, IA, 1989.

Elliot, Chandler H. *The Effective Student: A Constructive Method of Study.* Harper & Row, Publishers: New York, 1966.

Hawes, Gene R. and Hawes, Lynne Salop. *Hawes Guide to Successful Study Skills: How to Earn High Marks in York Courses and Tests.* New American Library: New York, 1981.

Herlin, Wayne R. and Albrecht, Laura J. *Study and Learning: The Development of Skill, Attitude And Style.* Kendall/Hunt Publishing Company: Dubuque, IA, 1990.

Huff, Darrell. *Score: The Strategy of Taking Tests.* Appleton-Century-Crofts: New York, 1961.

Kanar, Carol C. *The Confident Student,* 4th edition. Houghton Mifflin Company: New York, 2001.

Kessel-Turkel, Judi and Peterson, Franklynn. *Test Taking Strategies: How to Raise Your Score on All Types of Tests.* Contemporary Books, Inc.: Chicago, 1981.

Landsberger, Joe, site coordinator. Test Preparation and Taking Website, University of St. Thomas, St. Paul, Minnesota. 2004. http://www.iss.stthomas.edu/tstprp1.htm.

Maring, Gerald H., Burns, J. S. and Lee, Naomi P. *Mastering Study Skills: Making It Happen In College.* Kendall/Hunt Publishing Company: Dubuque, IA, 1988.

Starke, Mary C. *Strategies for College Success, Second Edition.* Prentice Hall: Englewood Cliffs, NJ, 1993.

Test Taking Strategies Website. Paul Treur, coordinator, University of Minnesota, Duluth. http://www.d.umm.edu/student/loon/acad/strat/test_take.html. 2004.

JOURNAL QUESTIONS

1. Now that you have reviewed this chapter, share your current methods that you use in preparing for tests. What methods do you need to modify and/or change? Remember, it's one thing to say and another to do.

2. Within the past week, how much time did you devote to test preparation? If you devoted any time at all to test preparation, what strategies did you use and why?

3. If you suffer from test anxiety, what strategies will you employ to reduce them. Discuss your plan of action.

Chapter 7

Critical Thinking

Developing Critical Skills for the Twenty-First Century

What are we to believe? What should we accept with reservations, and what should we dismiss outright? As we gather information about the world via the media (e.g., television, radio, the Internet, and newspapers and magazines), we tend to take much of the information at face value, ignoring the fact that the information has been selected and organized (shaped and edited) by the person or organization presenting it. People are often lulled into a false sense of security, believing that the sources of information they are basing their decisions on are objective and truthful (Chaffee, 1998). Discovering the answers to the six important questions that reporters are trained to answer near the beginning of every news article—who, what, where, when, why, and how—is not enough to allow us to think critically about complex and sometimes controversial topics. To engage in thinking at this higher level, one needs to know how to ask questions and think independently.

The authors of this chapter view critical thinking developmentally as a set of complex thinking skills that can be improved through knowledge and guided practice. Thinking skills are categorized in the problem-solving/decision-making set of life-skills necessary for information seeking. These skills include information assessment and analysis; problem identification, solution, implementation, and evaluation; goal setting; systematic planning and forecasting; and conflict resolution. Presented in this chapter are developmental thinking models, critical thinking and problem-solving models, and information about the construction and evaluation of an argument.

THINKING AS A DEVELOPMENTAL PROCESS

Cognitive psychologists study the development and organization of knowledge and the role it plays in various mental activities (e.g., reading, writing, decision making, and problem solving). What is knowledge? Where it is stored? How do you construct mental representations of your world? The personal answers to these and other questions are often found for the first time in college when students focus their attention on what they know and how they know it.

Models of Knowledge

Different forms of knowledge interact when you reason and construct a mental representation of the situation before you. Joanne Kurfiss (1988) wrote about the following three kinds of knowledge.

- **Declarative knowledge** is knowing facts and concepts. Kurfiss recognizes the considerable amount of declarative knowledge that students acquire through their college courses. To move students to a higher level of thinking, instructors generally ask students to write analytical essays, instead of mere summaries, to explain the knowledge they have acquired in the course.
- **Procedural knowledge,** or **strategic knowledge,** is knowing how to use declarative knowledge to do something (e.g., interpret textbooks, study, navigate the Internet, and find a major).
- **Metacognition** is knowing what knowledge to use to control one's situation (e.g., how to make plans, ask questions, analyze the effectiveness of learning strategies, initiate change). If students' metacognitive skills are not well developed, students may not be able to use the full potential of their knowledge when studying in college.

William Perry

You may have read about the developmental theorist William Perry. In his research on college-age students, Perry distinguished a series of stages that students pass through as they move from simple to complex levels of thinking. Basically, they move from *dualism*, the simplest stage, where knowledge is viewed as a factual quality dispensed by authorities (professors), to *multiplicity*, in which the student recognizes the complexity of knowledge (e.g., he or she understands that there is more than one perspective of the bombing of Hiroshima or the role of the United States in the Vietnam war) and believes knowledge to be subjective, to *relativism*, where the student reaches an understanding that some views make greater sense than other views. Relativism is reflected in situations where a student has made a commitment to the particular view they have constructed of the world, also known as *Weltanschauung*. Constructing a personal *critical epistemology* is an essential developmental task for undergraduates, according to Perry (Chaffee, 1998).

Bloom's Taxonomy of Thinking and Learning

Benjamin Bloom (1956) and his associates at the University of Chicago developed a classification system, or taxonomy, to explain how we think and learn (see Figure 1). The taxonomy consists of six levels of thinking arranged in a hierarchy, beginning with simple cognitive tasks (knowledge) and moving up to more complex thinking (evaluation). Thinking at each level is dependent on thinking skills at lower levels.

One of the reasons that college students often experience difficulty learning and studying during their first semester is that the learning and study strategies from high school are not necessarily effective in the new setting. In high school you are generally asked to memorize, comprehend, and interpret information. In college you are asked to do all that and more. To be successful in a college setting, you need to learn how to apply, analyze, synthesize, and evaluate information. Let's look at Bloom's six levels of learning and thinking.

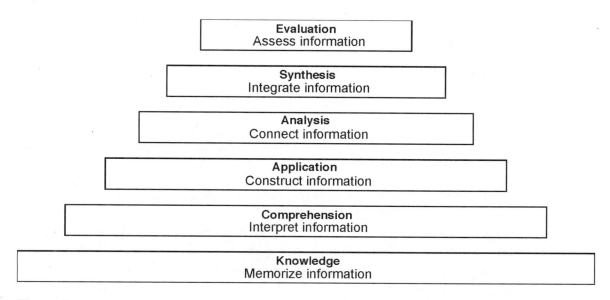

Figure 1 Bloom's Hierarchy of Thinking

Knowledge Level. If you are cramming for a test, chances are good that you are thinking at the knowledge level, the lowest level of thinking. You are basically attempting to memorize a lot of information in a short amount of time. If you are asked on the test to identify, name, select, define, or list particular bits of information, you might do okay, but you will most likely forget most of the information soon after taking the test.

Comprehension Level. When you are classifying, describing, discussing, explaining, and recognizing information, you are in the process of interpreting information. At the bottom of your lecture notes for the day, see if you can summarize your notes using your own words. In doing so, you can develop a deeper understanding of the material just covered in class.

Application Level. At this third level of thinking, you are constructing knowledge by taking previously learned information and applying it in a new and different way to solve problems. Whenever you use a formula or a theory to solve a problem, you are thinking at the application level. Some words used to describe how you process information at this level are *illustrate, demonstrate,* and *apply.* To increase thinking at the application level, develop the habit of thinking of examples to illustrate concepts presented in class or during reading. Be sure to include the examples in your notations in your books and notes.

Analysis Level. When you analyze information, you break the information down into parts and then look at the relationships among the parts. In your literature class, if you read two plays from different time periods and then compare and contrast them in terms of style and form, you are analyzing. When you analyze, you connect pieces of information. You *discriminate, correlate, classify,* and *infer.*

Synthesis Level. When you are synthesizing information, you are bringing together all the bits of information that you have analyzed to create a new pattern or whole. When you synthesize, you *hypothesize, predict, generate,* and *integrate.* Innovative ideas often emerge at the synthesis level of thinking.

Evaluation Level. This is the highest level of thinking according to Bloom's taxonomy. When you evaluate, you judge the validity of the information. You may be evaluating opinions ("Is that person really an expert?") or biases.

Answer the following questions to test your understanding of Bloom's taxonomy. According to Bloom's taxonomy of thinking, which level of thinking would you be engaging in if you were asked to

- Read an article about an upcoming candidate in a local election and then summarize the candidate's characteristics?
- View a video about hate and prejudice and then write an essay about how you can confront hate and prejudice on a personal level?
- Determine the most effective way for you to study?
- Identify and define the parts of the forebrain?
- Judge a new campus parking policy created by your college's parking services?

MODELS OF CRITICAL THINKING/ PROBLEM SOLVING

Critical Thinking

One of the primary objectives of a college education is to develop the skills necessary to become an autonomous, independent learner. Critical thinking prepares you to be an independent thinker. To ensure that you are thinking critically, you can follow the CRITICAL model developed by the authors (Glauser & Ginter, 1995). This model identifies important steps and key ideas in critical thinking: construction, refocus, identify, think through, insight, conclusions, accuracy, and lens.

Construction. Each of us constructs a unique view of the world. Our construction, or perception, of the world is based on our thoughts and beliefs. Our cultural background influences our perceptions, and they form the basis of our assumptions. For example, you might assume that a college education can help you to get a better job. How do you know this? Maybe you know this because a parent or teacher told you so. If this is the only bit of information on which you are basing your assumption about the value of a college education, you have not engaged in critical thinking. If you had engaged in critical thinking, you would have analyzed and synthesized information that you gathered about the benefits of a college education. If you have based your decision to attend this college on good critical thinking, then you will know why you are here and will more likely be motivated to graduate.

Perceptions of information, behaviors, and situations are often based on unexamined assumptions that are inaccurate and sketchy. The first step in this model is to investigate personal underlying biases that are inherent in your assumptions about any issue before you. For example, let us say that you are with some friends and the topic of surrogate motherhood comes up. Maybe you have already formed an opinion about the issue. This opinion could be based on strong critical thinking, but if not, then your opinion is merely a strong, personal feeling. If you choose to look at surrogate motherhood from a critical-thinking perspective, you would begin by examining your own thoughts and beliefs about motherhood and surrogacy. No matter what issue is before you (e.g., racism, abortion, euthanasia, genetic engineering), the process is the same; begin by examining your own assumptions. As you do this, look for biases and other patterns of thinking that have become cemented over time and are influencing the way you view the issue.

Refocus. Once you have acknowledged some of your own biases, refocus your attention so you can hear alternative viewpoints. Refocus by reading additional information, talking to people with opposing viewpoints, or maybe watching a movie or a video. You are trying to see other people's perspectives. Read carefully, and listen carefully with the intent to learn. Can you think of any books that you have read or movies that have influenced the way you see a particular issue?

To illustrate the effect of refocusing, list three sources of additional information (e.g., book, movie, another person, newspaper, or experience) that changed your mind about something important to you. Explain how it changed you.

1. _____

_____

_____

2. _____

_____

_____

3. _____

_____

_____

Identify. Identifying core issues and information is the third step of critical thinking. After you have gathered all your additional information representing different viewpoints, think over the information carefully. Are there any themes that emerge? What does the terminology related to the issue tell you? Look at all the facts and details. We all try to make sense out of what we hear and see by arranging information into a pattern, a story that seems reasonable. There is a tendency to arrange the information to fit our perceptions and beliefs. When we engage in critical thinking, we are trying to make sense of all the pieces, not just the ones that happen to fit our own preconceived pattern.

Think Through. The fourth step of critical thinking requires that you think through all the information gathered. The task is to distinguish between what is fact and what is fiction and what is relevant and not relevant. Examine premises and decide if they are logically valid. Look for misinformation. Maybe you have gathered inaccurate facts and figures. Check the sources for reliability. Asking questions is a large part of good critical thinking.

This step of the model is where you analyze and synthesize information. You are continually focusing your attention in and out, similar to the way you might focus a camera. This step of the critical-thinking process can be very creative. You are using both parts of the brain. The right brain is being speculative, suspending judgment, and challenging definitions. The left brain is analyzing the information received in a more traditional style, thinking logically and sequentially. While thinking critically, have you detected any over-generalizations (e.g., women are more emotional and less rational than men are) or over-simplifications (e.g., the high dropout rate at the local high school is due to an increase in single-parent families)?

Insight. Once key issues have been identified and analyzed, it is time to develop some insight into some of the various perspectives on the issue. Sometimes some of the best insights come when you can sit back and detach yourself from all the information you have just processed. Often new meanings will emerge that provide a new awareness. You might find that you have developed some empathy for others that may not have been there before. When you hear the term "broken home," what images do you conjure up? How do you think a child who resides with a single parent or alternates between divorced parents' homes feels when hearing that term applied to his or her situation? A lot of assumptions are embedded in such concepts.

Conclusions. If you do not have sufficient evidence to support a decision, suspend judgment until you do. An important tenet of critical thinking is not to jump to conclusions. If you do, you may find that you have a fallacy in your reasoning. A fallacy is an instance of incorrect reasoning. Maybe you did not have sufficient evidence to support your decision to major in biology, or maybe your conclusions about the issue of euthanasia do not follow logically from your premise. Also look at the conclusions you have drawn, and ask yourself if they have any implications that you might need to rethink? Do you need to consider alternative interpretations of the evidence?

Accuracy. You are not through thinking! In addition to looking for fallacies in your reasoning, you also need to consider some other things.

- Know the difference between reasoning and rationalizing. Which thinking processes are your conclusions based on?
- Know the difference between what is true and what seems true based on the emotional attachment you have to your ideas and beliefs.
- Know the difference between opinion and fact. Facts can be proven; opinions cannot.

Lens. In this last step of critical thinking, you have reached the understanding that most issues can be viewed from multiple perspectives. These perspectives form a lens that offers a more encompassing view of the world around you. Remember that there are usually many solutions to a single issue.

Problem Solving

Problem solving involves critical thinking. Are problem solving and critical thinking the same? Not really. Problem solving is about having the ability and skills to apply knowledge to pragmatic problems encountered in all areas of your life. If you were trying to solve a financial problem or decide whether or not to change roommates, you probably would not need a model of thinking as extensive as the one previously described. The following steps offer an organized approach to solving less complex problems.

1. Identify the problem. Be specific and write it down.
2. Analyze the problem.
3. Identify alternative ways to solve the problem.
4. Examine alternatives.
5. Implement a solution.
6. Evaluate.

Identify the problem. What exactly is the problem you wish to solve? Is it that your roommate is driving you crazy, or is it that you want to move into an apartment with your friend next semester? Be specific.

Analyze the problem. Remember, analysis means looking at all the parts. It is the process by which we select and interpret information. Be careful not to be too selective or simplistic in your thinking. Look at all the facts and details. For example, suppose you want to move into an apartment with your friends. Do you need permission from anyone to do so? Can you afford to do this? Can you get a release from your dorm lease? Your answer to all the questions might be yes, with the exception of being able to afford it. You want to move, so now the problem is a financial one. You need to come up with the financial resources to follow through on your decision.

Identify alternative ways to solve the problem. Use convergent and divergent thinking. You are engaging in **convergent thinking** when you are narrowing choices to come up with the correct solution (e.g., picking the best idea out of three). You are engaging in **divergent thinking** when you are thinking in terms of multiple solutions. Mihaly Csikszentmihalyi (1996) says, "Divergent thinking leads to no agreed-upon solution. It involves fluency, or the ability to generate a great quantity of ideas; flexibility, or the ability to switch from one perspective to another; and originality in picking unusual associations of ideas" (1996, p. 60). He concludes that a person whose thinking has these qualities is likely to come up with more innovative ideas.

Brainstorming is a great way to generate alternative ways to solve problems. This creative problem-solving technique requires that you use both divergent and convergent thinking. Here are some steps to use if you decide to brainstorm.

- Describe the problem.
- Decide on the amount of time you want to spend brainstorming (e.g., 10 minutes).
- Relax (remember some of the best insights come in a relaxed state).

- Write down everything that comes to your mind (divergent thinking).
- Select your best ideas (convergent thinking).
- Try one out! (If it does not work, try one of the other ideas you selected.)

Students have successfully used the process of brainstorming to decide on a major, choose activities for spring break, develop topics for papers, and come up with ideas for part-time jobs. Being creative means coming up with atypical solutions to complex problems.

Examine alternatives. Make judgments about the alternatives based on previous knowledge and the additional information you now have.

Implement a solution. Choose one solution to your problem and eliminate the others for now. (If this one fails, you may want to try another solution later.)

Evaluate. If the plan is not as effective as you had hoped, modify your plan or start the process over again. Also look at the criteria you used to judge your alternative solutions.

Think of a problem that you are currently dealing with. Complete Exercise 1 ("Creating Breakthroughs") at the end of the chapter. This is an opportunity to try to solve a problem using this six-step problem-solving model.

ARGUMENTS

Critical thinking involves the construction and evaluation of arguments. An argument is a form of thinking in which reasons (statements and facts) are given in support of a conclusion. The reasons of the argument are known as the **premises**. A good argument is one in which the premises are logical and support the conclusion. The validity of the argument is based on the relationship between the premises and the conclusion. If the premises are not credible or do not support the conclusion, or the conclusion does not follow from the premises, the argument is considered to be **invalid** or fallacious. Unsound arguments (based on fallacies) are often persuasive because they can appeal to our emotions and confirm what we want to believe to be true. Just look at commercials on television. Alcohol advertisements show that you can be rebellious, independent, and have lots of friends, fun, and excitement by drinking large quantities of alcohol—all without any negative consequences. Intelligence is reflected in the capacity to acquire and apply knowledge. Even sophisticated, intelligent people are influenced by fallacious advertising.

Invalid Arguments

> *It is human irrationality, not a lack of knowledge, that threatens human potential.*
> —Raymond Nickerson, in J. K. Kurfiss, *Critical Thinking*

In the book *How to Think About Weird Things*, Theodore Schick and Lewis Vaughn (1999) suggest that you can avoid holding irrational beliefs by understanding the ways in which an argument can fail. First, an argument is fallacious if it contains **unacceptable premises**, premises that are as incredible as the claim they are supposed to support. Second, if they contain **irrelevant premises**, or premises that are not logically related to the conclusion, they are also fallacious. Third, they are fallacious if they contain **insufficient premises**, meaning that the premises do not eliminate reasonable grounds for doubt. Schick and Vaughn recommend that whenever someone presents an argument, you check to see if the premises are acceptable, relevant, and sufficient. If not, then the argument presented is not logically compelling, or valid.

Schick and Vaughn abstracted from the work of Ludwig F. Schlecht the following examples of fallacies based on illogical premises.

Unacceptable Premises

- **False dilemma** (also known as the either/or fallacy) presumes that there are only two alternatives from which to choose when in actuality there are more than two. For example: You are either with America or against us. You are not with America, therefore you are against us.

- **Begging the question** is also referred to as arguing in a circle. A conclusion is used as one of the premises. For example: "You should major in business, because my advisor says that if you do, you will be guaranteed a job." "How do you know this?" "My advisor told me that all business majors find jobs."

Irrelevant Premises

- **Equivocation** occurs when the conclusion does not follow from the premises due to using the same word to mean two different things. For example: Senator Dobbs has always been *patriotic* and shown a deep affection and respect for his country. Now, though, he is criticizing the government's foreign policy. This lack of *patriotism* makes him unworthy of reelection.

- **Appeal to the person** (*ad hominem,* **or "to the man"**) occurs when a person offers a rebuttal to an argument by criticizing or denigrating its presenter rather than constructing a rebuttal based on the argument presented. As Schick and Vaughn note, "Crazy people can come up with perfectly sound arguments, and sane people can talk nonsense" (1999, p. 287).

- **Appeal to authority** is when we support our views by citing experts. If the person is truly an expert in the field for which they are being cited, then the testimony is probably valid. How often do you see celebrities endorsing products? Is an argument valid just because someone cites an article from the *New York Times* or the *Wall Street Journal* for support?

- **Appeal to the masses** is a type of fallacy that occurs when support for the premise is offered in the form, "It must be right because everybody else does it." For example: It's okay to cheat. Every college student cheats sometime during their undergraduate years.

- **Appeal to tradition** is used as an unsound premise when we argue that something is true based on an established tradition. For example: It's okay to drink large quantities of alcohol and go wild during Spring Break. It's what students have always done.

- **Appeal to ignorance** relies on claims that if no proof is offered that something is true, then it must be false, or conversely, that if no proof is offered that something is false, then it must be true. Many arguments associated with religions of the world are based on irrelevant premises that appeal to ignorance.

- **Appeal to fear** is based on a threat, or "swinging the big stick." For example: If you don't start studying now, you will never make it through college. Schick and Vaughn remind us, "Threats extort; they do not help us arrive at the truth" (1999, p. 289).

Insufficient Premises

- **Hasty generalizations** are often seen when people stereotype others. Have you noticed that most stereotypes are negative? When we describe an individual as pushy, cheap, aggressive, privileged, snobbish, or clannish and then generalize that attribute to the group we believe that person belongs to, we are committing a hasty generalization.
- **Faulty analogy** is the type of fallacy committed when there is a claim that things that have similar qualities in some respects will have similarities in other respects. For example: Dr. Smith and Dr. Wilson may both teach at the same college, but their individual philosophies about teaching and learning may be very different.
- **False cause** fallacies occur when a causal relationship is assumed despite a lack of evidence to support the relationship. Do you have a special shirt or hat that you wear on game days to influence the odds that the team you are cheering for wins?

CLOSING REMARKS

Belgian physicist Ilya Prigogine was awarded the Nobel Prize for his theory of dissipative structures. Part of the theory "contends that friction is a fundamental property of nature and nothing grows without it—not mountains, not pearls, not people. It is precisely the quality of fragility, he says, the capacity for being shaken up, that is paradoxically the key to growth. Any structure—whether at the molecular, chemical, physical, social, or psychological level that is insulated from disturbance is also protected from change. It becomes stagnant. Any vision—or any thing—that is true to life, to the imperatives of creation and evolution, will not be 'unshakable'" (Levoy, 1997 p. 8).

Throughout this textbook you will read about how change affects you now as a student in college and throughout the rest of your life. Education is about learning how to look and how to listen to what instructors, books, television, and other sources of information are saying, and to discover whether or not what they are saying is true or false.

In reference to education and learning, the philosopher Jiddu Krishnamurti said that there should be "an intent to bring about change in the mind which means you have to be extraordinarily critical. You have to learn never to accept anything which you yourself do not see clearly" (1974, p. 18). He said that education is always more than learning from books, or memorizing some facts, or the instructor transmitting information to the student. Education is about critical thinking, and critical thinking is the foundation of all learning.

Critical thinking is thinking that moves you beyond simple observations and passive reporting of those observations. It is an active, conscious, cognitive process in which there is always intent to learn. It is the process by which we analyze and evaluate information, and it is how we make good sense out of all the information that we are continually bombarded with.

Marcia Magolda believes that critical thinking fosters qualities such as maturity, responsibility, and citizenship. "Both the evolving nature of society and the student body has led to reconceptualizations of learning outcomes and processes. In a postmodern society, higher education must prepare students to shoulder their moral and ethical responsibility to confront and wrestle with the complex problems they will encounter in today and tomorrow's world. Critical, reflective thinking skills, the ability to gather and evaluate evidence, and the ability to make one's own informed judgments are essential learning outcomes if students are to get beyond relativity to make informed judgments in a world in which multiple perspectives are increasingly interdependent and 'right action' is uncertain and often in dispute." (Magolda & Terenzini, 1999, p. 3)

SOURCES

Bloom, B. (1956). *Taxonomy of educational objectives: The classification of educational goals. Handbook I: Cognitive domain.* London: Longmans.

Chaffee, J. (1998). *The thinker's way.* Boston: Little, Brown.

Csikszentmihalyi, M. (1996). *Creativity.* New York: HarperCollins.

DiSpezio, M. (1998). *Challenging critical thinking puzzles.* New York: Sterling.

Glauser, A., & Ginter, E. J. (1995, October). *Beyond hate and intolerance.* Paper presented at the southeastern Conference of Counseling Center Personnel, Jekyll Island, GA.

Johnson, D., & Johnson, F. (2000). *Joining together.* Boston: Allyn and Bacon.

Krishnamurti, J. (1974). *Krishnamurti on education.* New York: Harper & Row.

Kurfiss, J. G. (1988). *Critical thinking: Theory, research, practice, and possibilities. Critical thinking,* 2. Washington, DC: ASHE-Eric Higher Education Reports.

Levoy, Gregg. (1997). *Callings.* New York: Three Rivers Press.

Magolda, M. B., & Terenzini, P. (1999). Learning and teaching in the twenty-first century: Trends and implications for practice. In C. S. Johnson & H. E. Cheatham (Eds.), *Higher education trends for the next century: A research agenda for student's success.* Retrieved November 30, 1999, from http://www.acpa.nche.edu/ seniorscholars/trends/trends.htn

Perry, W. (1970). *Forms of intellectual and ethical development during the college years: A scheme.* New York: Holt, Rinehart and Winston.

Schick, T., & Vaughn, L. (1999). *How to Think About Weird Things: Critical Thinking for a New Age.* Mountain View, CA: Mayfield.

EXERCISE 1. CREATING BREAKTHROUGHS

Select a problem related to being a student at your college.

1. State the problem.

2. Analyze the problem.

3. Brainstorm alternative solutions.

4. Examine your alternatives. Pick the five best options from your brainstorming and record them below.

a. _____

b. _____

c. _____

d. _____

e. _____

When you consider your problem and the list of options that you have created, what kind of criteria do you want to use in judging your options? For example, let us say that you stated your problem as needing money to stay in school. The best five options you came up with for getting money to stay in school were to work full time and go to evening school, alternate between going to school for a year and then working for a year, take out a student loan, study hard and raise your GPA to obtain a scholarship, and beg your family for money. The criteria you choose to judge your options might be that you do not want to be really stressed out, you want your plan to be reliable, and you want to owe as little as possible upon graduation.

List three criteria you will use to evaluate your options.

C1. _____

C2. _____

C3. _____

Now, using a scale from 1–5, rate each option using your criteria, with 5 being the highest rating.

OPTIONS	C1	C2	C3	TOTAL (C1 + C2 + C3)
a.				
b.				
c.				
d.				
e.				

EXERCISE 1 (continued)

What are your two best options?

_____

_____

5. Implement a solution. Which option will you choose to act on?

_____

What kinds of resources will you need? (List four.)

_____

_____

_____

_____

List some of your planning steps.

_____

_____

_____

_____

_____

_____

_____

_____

_____

6. Evaluate. Look over what you have listed as resources and planning steps, and decide if you forgot something important. Indicate below if you believe the plan you have come up with is feasible, and whether you left something out that now should become part of your solution.

EXERCISE 2. CRITICAL-THINKING PUZZLE

Without lifting your pencil from the paper, draw six straight lines that connect all sixteen of the dots below. To make things more challenging, the line pattern that you create must begin at the X.

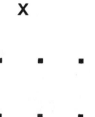

(The solution can be found at the end of this chapter.)

Source: DiSpezio, M. (1998). *Challenging critical thinking puzzles.* New York: Sterling.

Solution to Exercise 2

Critical-Thinking Puzzle

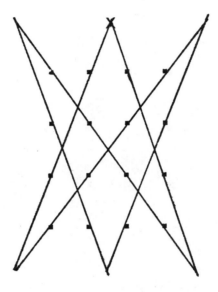

DiSpezio, M. (1998). *Challenging critical thinking puzzles.* New York: Sterling.

Chapter 8

Connecting Common Threads across a Diverse World

We live in an increasingly complex world that requires us to be adept in many life-skills (interpersonal communication/human relations, problem solving/decision making, physical fitness/health maintenance, and identity development/purpose-in-life). In a pluralistic society differences exist among and between various groups of people (e.g., ethnic, racial, religious, gender, sexual orientation, physical, and other groupings). While living in a pluralistic society can create tension as various groups attempt to sustain and develop their traditional culture or special interests within the confines of a common society, the experience can also create a rich source of energy that can fuel the creative potential of a society and advance it culturally and democratically. To fully develop as a person requires one to be aware of both the common threads that hold people together as a community, a nation, and a world and the unique threads of various hues and textures that complete the tapestry called humanity. It takes a multitude of skills to negotiate a diverse world.

MULTICULTURALISM

If we are to achieve a richer culture, rich in contrasting values, we must recognize the whole gamut of human potentialities, and so weave a less arbitrary social fabric, one in which each diverse human gift will find a fitting place.

—MARGARET MEAD

Multiculturalism is a philosophical belief based on ideals of social justice and equity that recognizes not only that diversity does exist but that it is a valuable resource in a community. Proponents of multiculturalism believe that it is to each and every person's advantage to acquire a set of skills, knowledge, and beliefs about diversity. These life-skills are needed individually to help us achieve success in a multicultural world and collectively to move our society beyond a toleration of differences among people to a respect for cultural pluralism.

Multiculturalism challenges us to recognize multiple perspectives, and in doing so, we enhance our problem-solving and critical-thinking skills. While adopting a multicultural perspective can prepare us to live in a multicultural world, it can also create discomfort, fear, denial, guilt, and anger during the process. People often believe that their own standards are the right standards; this view is known as *ethnocentricity*. When you have different groups of people living close to one another, and each group is functioning quite well by its own set of standards, conflict can arise as groups try to figure out what set of standards is right for the society as a whole.

College administrators understand that change is inevitable and recognize the value of a multicultural education in helping students to develop multicultural competencies. College campuses are a part of this multicultural world, and many colleges require students to take a multicultural class and, in addition, offer multidisciplinary programs (e.g., women's studies and African studies). As pointed out earlier, activities that challenge your mind expand the number and strength of neural connections that learning is based on. Engaging in activities that are unfamiliar or different (e.g., talking with people from cultures different from your own and engaging in diverse cultural experiences) helps to create a more complex system of thoughts, perceptions, assumptions, attitudes, feelings, and skills that can lead to a greater learning potential.

Manning Marable (2000) informs us that the racial composition of the United States is based on immigration, and that about a third of the total growth rate in the U.S. labor force is supplied by legal and illegal immigration. Pragmatically, students as well as others need to learn how to deal with diversity because the world in which we live is becoming more diverse. It is inevitable that among your neighbors, teachers, fellow students, coworkers, friends, and teammates will be individuals with backgrounds quite different from your own. You will need effective interpersonal skills to interact with these people. As a college student, you are in a unique learning situation that offers numerous opportunities to increase your diversity skills. If you have not formed relationships with people who have dissimilar backgrounds from you, now is your chance. People who ignore or resist opportunities may find themselves both vocationally and personally deficient in a global, multicultural society.

DEMOGRAPHIC CHANGES

The U.S. Bureau of the Census reported that in 2000 there were an estimated 281,421,906 million people living in the United States, an increase of 32.7 million people since the 1990 census. About 75.1 identified themselves as white only (down from 83% in 1990), 12.3% were black or African American only (down from 13% in 1990), 3.6% were Asian and Pacific American only, .9% were American Indian and Alaskan native only, and .1% were native Hawaiian and other Pacific Islander only. In addition, 5.5% identified themselves as some other race only, and about 2.4% selected more than one category. In response to a separate question on the census about ethnicity, 13% identified themselves as Hispanic or Latino, who may be of any race (up from 11% in 1990). The Hispanic or Latino population rose about 69% since 1990 (from 22.4 million to 35.3 million). Projections for the year 2050 are that the percentage of white people living in the United States will continue to decline and the percentage of current minorities will increase. The Hispanic or Latino population will show the largest increase (24%) followed by African Americans (15%). Today, most immigrants in this country come from Latin America, followed by Asia, and most immigrants settle in the western and southern parts of our nation. Some cities like Miami, where more than 59% of the population is foreign born, are more diverse than other cities.

Along with racial and ethnic demographic shifts there have been dramatic changes related to gender and age. Females (143,368,000) outnumbered males (138,054,000) in the United States in 2000, and women and minorities were identified as the largest groups of people to enter the work force. The *World Almanac* (2002) refers to the United States as an "aging nation" with a median age of 35.3, the highest ever reported. In 2000, it was estimated that there were about 4.2 million (1.5% of the total population) Americans 85 years or older and about 50,454 centenarians (people aged 100 and older) living in the United States. Centenarians have increased 35% in numbers since 1990. The 2000 census identified South Dakota, Iowa, and the District of Columbia as the states having the largest percentage of centenarians among their populations. What do you think accounts for such longevity? Researchers are looking for the answers as you read this.

Unfortunately, with the rise in diversity has also come a rise in the number of incidents related to prejudice and discrimination. According to the National Institute Against Prejudice and Violence (NIAPV), more than 250 of the nation's 3,300 colleges and universities have reported acts of violence against people due to their ethnicity since mid-1986.

LIVING IN A PLURALISTIC SOCIETY

Two primary goals of a college education are to help you develop life-long skills for continuous personal growth and to be a responsible community member. Today's college students do not believe that there are any quick fixes for our nation's social problems. One of the biggest social problems facing college students today on college campuses throughout the United States is racism. Racism is a form of discrimination based on biased assumptions about what people are and are not. It is a powerful force throughout the nation, weaving in and out of cultures, institutions, and individuals. Racism, ableism, sexism, heterosexism, ageism, and classism are all powerful discriminatory forces. These isms have the power to include, exclude, legitimize, and marginalize groups of people. Assumptions about what people are and are not enable prejudices and discrimination to flourish.

Throughout the world, countries are becoming more pluralistic. Diversity encompasses differences in educational level, gender, ethnicity, race, age, sexual orientation, religion, socioeconomic level, and physical ability. In the last 25 years there has been a dramatic shift in population trends in the United States, and the demographics of this country will continue to shift. The pluralities and complexities that exist between and among groups of people will also continue to change as differences in language, politics, regional differences, social class, religion and nationality further subdivide groups. Marable (2000) calls for a new and critical study of race and ethnicity to understand the changes that are taking place around us. He believes that one of the reasons that discussions about race and social diversity are so difficult is the complicated relationship between ethnicity and race.

TERMINOLOGY

The terminology associated with multiculturalism is continually changing to more accurately reflect changing attitudes about diversity. Currently you will read about "people of color" rather than nonwhites; gays, lesbians, and bisexuals rather than homosexuals; and people with disabilities rather than disabled or handicapped. Even though many people, through a process like stereotyping, choose to define you rather narrowly, most people choose to define themselves in broad, diverse categories. What comes to mind when you think of a nontraditional student? A fraternity member? A gay student? A Hispanic or Latino student? An Asian student? A student with disabilities? Culture refers to a way of being, the way we define ourselves. If someone asks you to define your culture, you might choose a narrow definition and respond that you are Catholic, Baptist, American, or German. You might also choose a broader definition of culture and respond that you are a musician, a Southerner, an athlete, or a member of a sorority.

What about race? Is it a social concept used to discriminate against groups of people or is it a biological/genetic concept? There is a lot of controversy in the literature about the definition of race. Pedersen (1994) defines race as "a pseudobiological system of classifying persons by a shared genetic history or physical characteristics such as skin color" (p. x). Race is a topic that people struggle to talk about with one another. Talking about race can be especially challenging due to the political and emotional misapplications of the term. For the first time in the history of the census, respondents in 2000 were given the choice of selecting one or more race categories to identify their racial identity. About 2.4% (6.8 million) of the total population chose more than one category of race. Questions about being Hispanic or Latino were designated a separate category. As pointed out previously, there is often more diversity within a group of people who are regarded as having similar characteristics than there is between different groups.

Ethnicity exists within the broader category of race. Ethnic groups such as Japanese, Cambodian, Chinese, Korean, Filipino, Vietnamese, and Pacific Islander fall under the racial umbrella of Asian. Hispanics, or Latinos, as some people prefer, are Spanish-speaking people. Some Hispanic people may be from Puerto Rico, the Dominican Republic, Mexico, Cuba, Colombia, or Argentina. Hispanics are a very diverse group with varied customs, food, cultural patterns, and politics. People who refer to themself as black might look to Africa, Haiti, Jamaica, or the West Indies for their cultural heritage. People who identify with having a white ethnic background may look to Poland, Australia, Italy, Africa, Ireland, or Germany. Among the American Indian and Alaska native population, you will also find a multiplicity of cultural patterns.

Before you read about suggestions for developing multicultural competencies, in the next section, take a moment to become familiar with some of the terms associated with diversity and multiculturalism.

ableism	prejudice or discrimination against people with mental, emotional, and physical disabilities
ageism	prejudice or discrimination based on age
anti-Semitism	hostility toward Jewish people
classism	prejudice or discrimination based on economic background
culture	group of people bound together by traditions (food, language, religion) and values
discrimination	an action or policy that differentiates one group from another in terms of treatment

ethnocentrism	a belief that one's own culture is more correct or superior
homophobia	an irrational fear of gays, lesbians, or bisexuals
prejudice	preconceived opinion for or against someone or something
privilege	unearned access to resources due to membership in a particular social group
racism	discrimination based on skin color and ethnicity; a belief that a particular race is superior or inferior
sexism	prejudice or discrimination based on gender
stereotyping	overgeneralizing about groups of people based on biased assumptions

DEVELOPING MULTICULTURAL COMPETENCIES

We know that our attitudes and beliefs influence our perceptions. We assimilate attitudes and beliefs throughout our lives, forming assumptions about the way things are and are not, including judgments about people. Unfortunately, we tend to filter out information that does not affirm, or align with, our perception of the world, so we tend to rely on many biased assumptions to guide us through life. Biased assumptions distort the truth and give rise to prejudices that keep us confined in narrowly defined spaces. Is there any way for us to get out of our own little boxes to see what is truly going on around us? The answer is, emphatically, yes! Biases can be intentional or unintentional. They might be based on cultural isolation or ignorance. When you form a belief about an entire group of people without recognizing individual differences among members of the group, you are engaging in *stereotyping*.

We are all guilty of stereotyping because of the way in which the mind stores, organizes, and recalls information to reduce complexity and help us make quick decisions (Johnson & Johnson, 2000). Johnson and Johnson report that the term stereotype was initially used in the eighteenth century to describe a printing process that duplicated pages of type. According to Johnson and Johnson (2000) it was not until 1922 that Walter Lippman used the term to describe the process by which people gloss over details to simplify social perceptions. We tend to stereotype people to whom we do not pay much attention. The practice of stereotyping can lead to prejudice, which can lead to discrimination.

What can you do to overcome biases that cloud your perceptions and create distortions? How do you move beyond intolerance and prejudice? These are questions that have no easy answers. Examining your own attitudes, becoming more aware of other cultures, and developing a multicultural view that will help you communicate, appreciate, and respect people from diverse backgrounds are steps in the right direction.

Examine Your Attitudes

Your culture surrounds you. Culture influences the way you think, feel, and behave. Identities are forged within the cultural context in which you live. Society, the larger culture in which you live, sends both positive and negative messages about the self. Unconscious or conscious beliefs about the way you are suppose to be can create a great deal of pain for those who are excluded and marginalized by the majority members of society. If while you were growing up you received a constant stream of negative messages that you were not okay because your cultural rules were different from those in the dominant culture, you may have internalized feelings that you are not okay. Prejudice has a negative impact on the process of identity formation. Examine some of your own prejudices by answering the questions in Exercise 1.

Attitudes can create barriers to interacting with people from diverse backgrounds. When you see someone walking toward you, what do you tend to notice? Gender? Weight? Skin color? Clothing? Hair? What kinds of assumptions do you make based on your observations? Student? Sorority girl? Nontraditional student? Professor? Athlete? Foreigner? Finally, what assumptions do you make about each kind of person? We all assume things about people. Just remember that your assumptions are often incorrect. Prejudice is a learned habit, and it takes a conscious effort to break it.

Sources of Prejudice

Where do these prejudices come from? They come from a variety of sources.

Economic Competitiveness and Scapegoating. Scapegoating is the process of displacing aggression or projecting guilt onto a group of people. When the economy is bad, accusations like "Those immigrants are taking away all our jobs" increase in frequency. Political candidates sometimes appeal to prejudices among voters. They may scapegoat immigrants, for example, in an effort to win votes from those who feel disempowered or frustrated with the economy.

Parents and Relatives. What messages did your parents send about other people? When you were young and found yourself near a person in a wheelchair, what messages did you receive about how to behave? Did you observe the adult look away or maybe address the person accompanying the person with the disability rather than communicating directly with the person who was disabled? What about when you asked a parent if a friend who was from another socioeconomic or cultural group could come home with you or if you could go to his or her house? Messages can be overt or covert. The effect is the same. When negative messages are attached to differences between people, prejudice takes root.

Institutions. Prejudice is learned through living in a society where prejudices are sustained. Who received the most privileges in your school? Did the gifted students get to engage in more creative learning situations than the other students? What about overweight children in your school? How were they treated? Who participated in sports and organizations with you? Were accommodations made for someone who was mentally or physically disabled? As a child, were you ever conscious of the fact that all U.S. presidents have been white males?

Media. What kinds of messages do you receive from magazines, movies, and television? What prejudices are perpetuated in the media? What groups of people are stereotyped? What types of misinformation about certain groups of people are broadcast? When you watch television or go to a movie, how are women depicted? How often are they depicted as sex symbols? Stereotyping is based on ignorance. Have you heard any disparaging remarks about others lately through the media? What about jokes about religion, sexual orientation, skin color, or weight?

Social Fragmentation. Levine and Cureton (1998) found that undergraduate students across the country described themselves more in terms of differences than similarities. Their study also revealed that students today are more socially isolated than previous generations; increasingly, they voluntarily segregate themselves to form small self-interest groups. Look around you. Do gaps between socioeconomic groups in this country seem to be widening?

The sources that fuel prejudice come together to create a powerful, destructive force that can lead to discrimination and even violence. The number of reported incidents of prejudice and discrimination are reported to be on the rise throughout the country. The Anti-Defamation League and the National Institute Against Prejudice and Violence (NIAPV) record and report incidents of prejudice, discrimination, and hate crimes. The brutal murders of Matthew Shepard, a gay, white man who was a student at the University of Wyoming, and James Byrd, Jr., a black man who was chained to the back of a pickup truck and dragged to his death, outraged the country. Yet *Life* magazine reported that at Matthew Shepard's funeral, a protestor appeared with a sign that read "God hates fags."

The Power of Prejudice

Ableism. Joy Weeber (1999), a person with a disability, has written about being discriminated against and described how painful it is. She wrote that her pain was caused by unconscious beliefs of a society that assume that everyone is, or should be, normal, . . . "capable of total independence and pulling themselves up by their own bootstraps" (p. 21). She defined ableism as a form of prejudice and bigotry that has as its core a belief in the superiority of being nondisabled and an assumption that those who are disabled wished they could be nondisabled—at any cost.

Laura Rauscher and Mary McClintock (1998) offer the following comments to help educate people about disability and oppression.

- Disability is not inherently negative.
- Becoming disabled involves major life changes including loss as well as gain, but it is not the end of a meaningful and productive existence.
- People with disabilities experience discrimination, segregation, and isolation as a result of other people's prejudice and institutional ableism, not because of the disability itself.
- Social beliefs, cultural norms, and media images about beauty, intelligence, physical ability, communication, and behavior often negatively influence the way people with disabilities are treated.
- Societal expectations about economic productivity and self-sufficiency devalue persons who are not able to work, regardless of other contributions they may make to family and community life.
- Without positive messages about who they are, persons with disabilities are vulnerable to internalizing society's negative messages about disability.

- Independence and dependence are relative concepts, subject to personal definition, something every person experiences, and neither is inherently positive or negative.
- The right of people with disabilities to inclusion in the mainstream of our society is now protected by law, yet they are still not treated as full and equal citizens.

Heterosexism. Heterosexism is the belief that heterosexuality is the only acceptable sexual orientation. In recent years in the United States, there has been increased visibility, via news coverage, movies, advertisements, and television, of gay, lesbian, and bisexual people. Pat Griffin and Bobbie Harro (1997) point out that despite the increased visibility, most Americans continue to have contradictory feelings about gay, lesbian, and bisexual people, and that educators have been uncommonly reluctant to address the issue of homophobia in the schools. Silence about issues that minimize particular groups of people can have devastating effects. The Department of Health and Human Services Report on teen suicide (1989) indicated that lesbian, gay, and bisexual young people are two to three times more likely to commit suicide. Prejudice and discrimination are powerful forces that isolate and marginalize people in society. The first step to getting beyond prejudice and intolerance is to examine your own attitudes and beliefs about people. The second step is to develop an awareness of other cultures.

Developing an Awareness of Other Cultures. Educate yourself about issues related to multiculturalism. Make an effort to get to know people from dissimilar backgrounds. Your college probably hosts a variety of cultural events throughout the year. Many international student organizations sponsor cultural nights, which students and the community are invited to attend. Discover when they are and make a commitment to be there. Develop an open mind, like an anthropologist observing other cultures. As you begin to observe other cultures, be aware of your own cultural filters.

Colleges offer opportunities to study abroad. If your college does not offer a study program in a country you wish to visit, check with other colleges and see what they have to offer. Immerse yourself in different cultures. Ask lots of questions. Learn about different international organizations on campus and in your community. Also check with your local Chamber of Commerce for local cultural celebrations.

You can also educate yourself about other cultures by watching videos. Try renting some international movies the next time you pick up a video at your local video rental store. Having to read subtitles cannot be used as an excuse! Your aim is to become more immersed in another culture. You might also try attending a different place of worship or interviewing other students about their experiences living in a different culture. The more personal information you have about another person or another culture, the less likely you are to stereotype that person or culture.

DEVELOPING A MULTICULTURAL VIEW

Developing a multicultural view requires the motivation to develop better diversity skills to interact with a wider range of people. For some people, the motivation to become multi-culturally competent arises from a desire to become a social change agent in the community by helping other people develop more tolerant attitudes. Some people view this as a way of supporting their country, since democracy is a system based on mutual respect and equality of rights. There are things you can do to help build a healthier approach to living in a multicultural society.

Develop Good Critical-Thinking Skills. Learn to think through your assumptions about different groups of people. Remember that your assumptions are based on your experiences. Since your experiences are necessarily limited, your assumptions are going to have many biases where you filled in the gaps. The process of critical thinking can help you get beyond preconceived notions that have been formulated over the years and see the truth.

Part of the process of developing good critical thinking skills is becoming aware of the influence you have on other people. Starting with yourself, think of how you influence friends and family, people at work and school, and your community. What actions could you implement within each one of these spheres to combat sexism, racism, ableism, and other discriminatory isms? How can you change your environment to encourage a multicultural view of the world?

Educate Others about Laws and Policies. There are campus policies and laws to deal with acts of bigotry and discrimination. Become familiar with them. What kind of sexual harassment policy does your college enforce? In 1990 the Americans with Disabilities Act (ADA), a civil rights act for people with disabilities, passed into law. It states that all public facilities, including colleges, are required by law to make a serious effort to provide barrier-free access to all persons with disabilities. When you are eating out in a restaurant, do you ever wonder whether or not the restaurant you are dining in is accessible to all? Many restaurants and public places are not. How does your college respond to incidents of bigotry? Bigotry can appear in many forms: graffiti, physical violence, written and spoken remarks, and privileges. What about invited or uninvited outside speakers who come to campus to speak with students? Should a student newspaper be allowed to run an advertisement that provides misinformation about a group of people and promotes racism, sexism, anti-Semitism, or any other form of intolerance? What about running a cartoon that is demeaning to people with disabilities in a campus, local, or national newspaper?

The issue of political correctness (PC) has been debated on campuses and throughout society. Pedersen (1994) states, "Philosophically, PC means the subordination of the right to free speech to the right of guaranteeing equal protection under the law. The PC position contends that an absolutist position on the First Amendment (that you may slur anyone you choose) imposes a hostile environment for minorities and violates their right to equal education. Promotion of diversity is one of the central tenets of PC" (p. 5). Are you an advocate or proponent of PC? Why? Or why not?

SOURCES

Barron, W. G. (2002). United States population: Census 2000—The results start rolling in. In W. A. McGeveran (Ed.), *The world almanac and book of facts 2002* (pp. 374–385). New York: World Almanac Books.

Glauser, A., & Bozarth, J. D. (2001). Person-centered counseling: The culture within. *Journal of Counseling & Development, 79,* 142–147.

Glauser, A. (1999). Legacies of racism. *Journal of Counseling & Development, 77,* 62–67.

Glauser, A. (1996). *Dangerous habits of the mind: Getting beyond intolerance and prejudice.* Presentation made at the 1996 World Conference of the American Counseling Association, Pittsburgh, PA.

Goodman, D., & Schapiro, S. (1997). Sexism curriculum design. In Adams, M., Bell, L., & Griffin, P. (Eds.). *Teaching for diversity and social justice: A sourcebook* (pp. 110–140). New York: Routledge.

Griffin, P. & Harro, B. (1997). Heterosexism curriculum design. In Adams, M., Bell, L., & Griffin, P. (Eds.). *Teaching for diversity and social justice: A sourcebook* (pp. 141–169). New York: Routledge.

Johnson, D., & Johnson, F. (2000). *Joining together.* Boston: Allyn and Bacon.

Levine, A., & Cureton, J. S. (1998). *When hope and fear collide.* San Francisco: Jossey-Bass.

Life: The year in pictures, 1998. (1999). New York: Time.

Marable, M. (February 25, 2000). We need new and critical study of race and ethnicity. *Chronicle of Higher Education*, B4–B7.

Pedersen, P. (1994). *A handbook for developing multicultural awareness.* Alexandria, VA: American Counseling Association.

Princeton Language Institute. (1993). *Twenty-first century dictionary of quotations.* New York: Dell.

Rauscher, L., & McClintock, M. (1997). Ableism curriculum design. In Adams, M., Bell., L., & Griffin, P. (Eds.). *Teaching for diversity and social justice: A sourcebook* (pp. 198–230). New York: Routledge.

U.S. Department of Health and Human Services. (1989). *Report of the Secretary's Task Force on Youth Suicide.* Rockville, MD: Author.

Weeber, J. E. (1999). What could I know of racism? *Journal of Counseling & Development, 77,* 20–23.

Wijeyesinghe, C. L., Griffin, P., & Love, B. (1997). Racism curriculum design. In Adams, M., Bell, L. & Griffin, P. (Eds.). *Teaching for diversity and social justice: A sourcebook* (pp. 82–109). New York: Routledge.

NAME: _____ **DATE:** _____

EXERCISE 1. ASSESSING CULTURAL INFLUENCES

1. When were you first aware of differences among people?

2. When did you become aware of your own racial/ethnic heritage?

3. When did you first experience some form of prejudice? Do you remember your thoughts and feelings?

4. When did you become aware that you had certain privileges, or that you were denied privileges, based on your physical characteristics, socioeconomic background, or ability level?

5. How have others stereotyped you or members of your family?

6. What kinds of messages did you receive as a child that you were inferior or superior to others? Who or what sent these messages?

EXERCISE 2. REFLECTING ON RACE RELATIONS

1. Do you think that only certain groups of people are racist? Give examples.

2. How can your college better recruit minorities to enroll at your college?

3. What are race relations like in your community? What about on campus?

4. How can you constructively confront prejudice and discrimination on a personal level?

5. If you were in a position of authority, what could you do to bring your community together to celebrate diversity?

Chapter 9

Planning for a Career

MAKING CAREER DECISIONS

Making career decisions is a lifelong task. You have already begun the process by deciding to go to college. The courses you take, your choice of major, the work experience you accumulate, the clubs and groups you join, and the people you meet may influence the career decisions you make in your lifetime.

Chances are you are already thinking about your choice of major and related career options. Don't be alarmed if you feel uncertain or have no ideas about your career plans. Now is the time to question, explore, and wonder. It can be reassuring to know that many sources of career information and systems of career decision-making already exist to help you in this task.

Before we get into a discussion of what goes into career decision-making, let's explore some popular myths that might sabotage your efforts to make informed decisions.

CAREER MYTHS

1. "I don't need to think about my career now; I'm just starting college."
    Graduation may be years away—but the process of career-planning has already begun. Knowing who you are and what you are looking for will better enable you to find satisfying career options. And self-assessment takes time!

2. "I want to take **THAT TEST** that will tell me what I should be."
    There is **NO** test that will tell you what you should be or what career you should follow. Different types of career assessments can be useful in gathering information about you and relating it to career clusters. Test results often help you to put information in order so you can verify or challenge your ideas. These assessments are tools; the decision is yours.

3. "I'll pursue whatever career is in demand."
    Knowing what's "hot" in the job market is important information, but not the only information you need to make a decision. Without knowing about your own interests and skills, you may choose a career that's available, but later you may find you are not suited for it.

4. "I need to find the perfect career."
   There is no "perfect" career. What you will discover is that there are several ways you can find a meaningful career. No one gets 100 percent of what she wants. There is usually compromise. Your task is to identify what you want and need from your career, put these features into priority, and use this information as a guide in making your career decisions.

5. "If I make the wrong decision, I'll be stuck forever."
   Fear of making the wrong decision can prevent you from making *any* decision. When making career decisions, you'll find that nothing is written in stone. Few people head into one career and stay there for their whole working lives. The U.S. Bureau of Labor Statistics estimates that the average worker will change careers five times during a work life.

6. "Everyone knows what major/career they want but me."
   It may seem like everyone is decided but you. However, statistics show that most students change majors (and career plans) several times while in college. It is better to recognize that you are undecided, and go about finding the necessary information to make your decisions, than to assume you have it all figured out and never evaluate your plan.

CAREER/LIFE PLANNING PROCESS

So, how do you get started with career planning? Let's begin with a definition of the Career/Life Planning Process, which involves three components:

Career/Life

Your career decisions will include more than which job to take upon graduation. Your career is the sum of all the work experiences you will have. The work you choose to pursue will have a direct impact on the way you live your life. Your career decisions cannot be made in a vacuum, but should be made within the context of your lifestyle preferences.

Planning

Webster defines planning as "formulating a program to accomplish or attain something." It is purposeful and done ahead of time. Therefore, career/life planning implies setting short- and long-range goals about your work and lifestyle with specific objectives that will help you meet them.

Process

Your career plan will not be the result of one decision you make, but rather a series of decisions throughout your lifetime. You will go through the steps in career planning several times because as you continue to grow and develop as a person, your interests, skills, and values will also change. The job market definitely changes, sometimes beyond your control. So "process" implies a dynamic aspect of developing satisfying and successful career and life plans.

The whole process might seem overwhelming, but the career/life planning process can be broken down into three basic steps with specific tasks to accomplish. The following diagram is a picture of this process:

STEP ONE: UNDERSTANDING YOURSELF REQUIRES SELF-ASSESSMENT

Knowing about yourself is the basis of career decision-making. This includes identifying your interests—what you like and dislike; your skills—what you do well; your values—what is important to you about your work; and your personality traits or characteristics—how you behave as a person.

The exercises at the end of the chapter help you to start the self-assessment process.

Analyze Your Experiences

A good method for analyzing what you have already done is to consider your accomplishments. These experiences do not have to be grand, such as a cure for cancer or the answer to world peace, or fit anyone else's definition of accomplishment. The accomplishments should be something you feel good about from your life (college, work, leisure, relationships). These are usually experiences that presented a challenge and satisfaction in achieving, such as:

- passing chemistry
- running a 10K race
- volunteering in a nursing home
- researching the family tree
- being elected Student Body President

VALUES

Values identify what is important to you. Work values describe what is important about the work you do. It is useful to identify values when considering possible careers because they may tell you about work-related needs, motivators, and long-term satisfaction.

Do you notice a pattern or relationship among your interests, skills, values, and personality traits? What implications might these similarities have on careers that might be interesting to you? Share your insights with someone who knows you and compare notes.

Learn to evaluate all of your experiences—work, school, and hobbies—on a regular basis. This process can turn up characteristics you might find satisfying in your future career. And remember, identifying what you don't want can be as helpful as finding what you do want. Both help define what you are looking for.

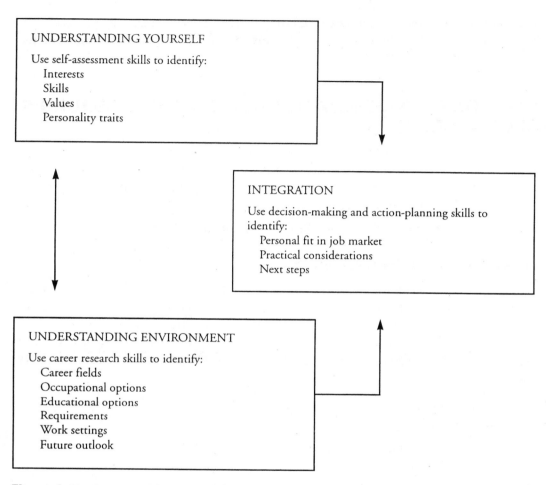

Figure 1 The Process of Career/Life Planning

STEP TWO: CONDUCTING CAREER RESEARCH

The U.S. Bureau of Labor classifies over 20,000 different occupations. These occupations are often grouped into career clusters that share similar job functions, skills, or training requirements. It's impossible to know about every job that's in the workforce, but you should be familiar with the general categories such as:

Agriculture/Home Economics
Arts/Humanities
Business
Education/Welfare
Engineering/Architecture
Government/Law
Health
Industry/Trade

Services

Science

The following list of career references can help you explore specific occupations in each cluster. You can find these reference books in the university library, the Career Services office, or any public library.

Dictionary of Occupational Titles

Published by the U.S. Department of Labor, gives standardized and comprehensive descriptions of job duties and related information for 20,000 occupations. Each job title has a nine-digit code number.

Occupational Outlook Handbook

Published by the U.S. Department of Labor, describes what workers do on the job, working conditions, the training and education needed, earnings, expected job prospects.

Occupational Outlook Quarterly

Published by the U.S. Department of Labor. This magazine offers articles featuring various occupations. The **Quarterly** often features unusual, interesting, overlooked possibilities. One issue per year reviews job prospects for all major occupations.

Guide for Occupational Exploration

Published by JIST for the U.S. Department of Labor, describes 2,500 job titles by interest, skills required, and industry. It is cross-referenced to other career books.

Encyclopedia of Careers

Published in four volumes by J.G. Ferguson Publishing Co., describes careers by general categories such as professional, technical, special fields. Also included are industry profiles.

Internet Sources

There are many electronic sources for career-related information. Since actual Website addresses can change frequently, try starting with a keyword search using the word "career," or enter the career you are interested in, followed by "employment."

As you conduct your research, be sure to locate the following information:

Job description

Skills required

Training (educational level/major/degree/license, etc.)

Work environment

Salary projections

Future outlook

Related occupations

STEP THREE: INTEGRATION REQUIRES DECISION-MAKING AND ACTION PLANNING

This is probably the most important step because integration requires taking what you know about yourself and putting it together with the reality of the work world. In doing so, you begin to identify and evaluate career options that are practical for you. Questions to consider:

- What career clusters am I interested in?
- What career fields are found in these clusters?
- What specific occupations are found in these career fields?
- What type of preparation is needed for these jobs?
- Does the university offer these programs of study?
- Do I have the academic strengths to pursue that major?
- What challenges might be presented in the job market (competition, relocation)?
- Do I have the time, money, and support resources to pursue these options?
- What else do I need to know in order to identify my career objective?

Gathering and evaluating information is a critical part of choosing a major and making career plans. Here are some additional information resources:

Career Services

Most campus Career Service offices provide career advising, career reference materials, employer literature, and job search information. Computerized career guidance programs, such as SIGI Plus, DISCOVER, or CHOICES, are excellent tools for self-assessment and career exploration. Services might also be available for student employment, internships, resume writing, interview preparation, and Internet searches.

Informational Interviewing

Another way to get information is to talk to people about their jobs. This can be on a casual basis, such as talking with family and friends, or it can be done in a formal way by contacting experienced professionals in your field of interest and scheduling an appointment to meet with them. Either way, you are interviewing for information. This technique is an excellent way to get inside information that might not be available in written sources. It also helps you to develop your communication skills and a professional network, which you will need in your future career. Try the following exercise to gather career information and practice your interviewing skills.

Experience

After you have gathered substantial information, the next thing to do is test your ideas through some first-hand experience. Many people find they learn best by doing; this is described as experiential learning. Experiential learning programs include Cooperative Education, Internships, and career-related volunteer work. Work experience helps you get a first-hand look at your intended career field. This realworld opportunity will allow you to develop experience for your resume, meet employers, apply what you are learning in the classroom, and evaluate the fit of this career. Participation in experiential learning programs is usually competitive, and requires planning. Think about making it part of your college agenda. Contact the Career Service office at your college for more information.

Summary

As you can see, there are many career-planning tasks you can be working on during your first year. Remember the three steps in the process: Self-Assessment, Career Research, and Decision Making/Action Planning. "Your College Guide for Career Success" (Figure 2) will serve as a handy guide and reminder of career-related things to do during your college program. It also provides suggestions for making and implementing your career plans for the future. Start using it!

FRESHMAN

Explore Career Areas

Visit campus career center
  for orientation on programs & services
Talk with parents, friends, professors, and
  counselor about your career ideas
Complete career assessments
Identify the following:
  interests
  abilities
  career-related hobbies
  personality style
  career values

SOPHOMORE

Collect Information

Research careers in the library
Conduct info interview
List 5 career options for your intended majors
Select electives to test career ideas
Confirm major
Explore experiential options to test career skills
  and ideas

JUNIOR

Increase experience

Apply for Intern/Co-op assignment
Develop your resume
Attend Law/Grad school info fair
Take leadership role in student club/group
Attend career fairs

SENIOR

Implement Career Plan

Register with Career Services office
Attend training session on:
  Resume/Cover letter writing
  Interviewing skills
  Resume critique
Develop list of targeted employers
Send out graduate school applications
Network, network, network

Figure 2 Your College Guide for Career Success

EXERCISE 1. IDENTIFY YOUR INTERESTS

By answering the questions below you will start to highlight activities you enjoy.

1. What subjects do you like?

2. What books or magazines do you read?

3. What do you like to do for fun? What do you do in your spare time?

4. What jobs have you had? What did you like or dislike about them? (Remember to include volunteer work.)

5. Based on your responses, write a short statement about the things you like to do, and why. What types of activities are included or excluded?

EXERCISE 2. ACCOMPLISHMENTS

Identify five accomplishments. Write a short description of each, including the situation, your actions, and the outcome. What challenges did you face? How did you overcome them?

1.

2.

3.

4.

5.

Now, select three of your accomplishments. List each one on a separate piece of paper. Complete this part of your self-assessment by answering the following questions regarding each accomplishment:

- What skills did you use?

- How did you interact with people?

- Did you work alone or with others?

- Did it require you to be a leader or team member?

- How did you deal with data, ideas, and/or things?

- Which did you enjoy the most?

- What was most difficult?

- What was most rewarding?

- How much structure was involved?

- What interests are represented? Art, music, sports, travel, animals, science, etc.?

- What values are represented? Helping society, competition, influencing people, fame, self-expression, excitement, etc.?

EXERCISE 3. VALUES CHECKLIST

Following is a partial list of work values, with an example of each. Read the list and examples of each value when applied to work settings. Rate each value according to the scale below.

Rate each work value: V if it is very important; S if it is somewhat important; or N if it is not important.

Adventure	take risks in work
Creativity	developing new ideas or things
Authority	being in charge
Altruism	helping others
Independence	plan own work schedule/work without close supervision
Travel	opportunities to travel on the job
Prestige	be recognized and respected for the work I do
Stability	keep a routine without surprises
Variety	experience change and enjoy different tasks
Family	have time and energy to spend with family
Teamwork	work as a member of a team
Learning	opportunity to learn new skills and apply them on the job
Challenge	use your skills and abilities to solve complex problems
Advancement	opportunity for promotion
Leisure	have time out of work to pursue other interests
Wealth	have a high income

Of course, just identifying what you want is not realistic. There is no guarantee that you will be able to satisfy all of the values that are very important to you. Compromise will be a necessity. From your list of Very Important values, choose five that you believe are most important (probably things you will not be able to live without). Now prioritize these five values on the list below.

1.

2.

3.

4.

5.

NAME: _____ **DATE:** _____

EXERCISE 4. DESCRIBE YOURSELF

List 10 words that describe you.

1.   6.

2.   7.

3.   8.

4.   9.

5.   10.

Which words identify work-related strengths or assets?

Which identify work-related weaknesses or liabilities?

EXERCISE 5. PERSONAL CAREER PROFILE

Use this space to summarize your self-information.

Interests:

List three interests you have identified:

1.

2.

3.

List three activities or things you wish to avoid:

1.

2.

3.

List three skills you feel are your strengths:

1.

2.

3.

List three work-related values:

1.

2.

3.

List three personality traits:

1.

2.

3.

Write a short statement describing your "ideal" job.

EXERCISE 6. ORGANIZING AN INFORMATIONAL INTERVIEW

First, start with relatives, friends, and co-workers, or referrals from people you know. If you feel comfortable, identify people in positions of interest in your community and formally contact them for an Informational Interview. If you are contacting strangers, you might begin by introducing yourself as a college student doing research on (your career of interest). Most people are willing to talk about what they do; just be sure to respect their time and busy schedule. Therefore, always have your questions prepared in advance and arrive on time.

Next, develop questions for your Informational Interview. Feel free to add new questions to this sample list. Once you begin the interview, record the responses for processing later.

• How did you decide upon this occupation?

• What are your major responsibilities on the job?

• What is your typical day like?

• What do you like best about the work you do? What do you like least?

• What are the latest trends in this field?

• What training and skills are necessary for a career in this area?

• What advice would you give to someone who is planning for a career in this field?

• Can you recommend someone else whom I should talk to in this field?

Finally, write a short summary of your experience. What did you learn that might help you in planning for your career?

Appendix

1. University Vocabulary

ADMINISTRATORS' TITLES

1.	Chancellor	highest officer of our regional campus
2.	Vice Chancellor	4 V.C.'s; managers of 4 main divisions
3.	Asst. Vice Chancellor	assigned specific areas within divisions
4.	Dean of Students	manages student issues re: discipline, probation, dismissal
5.	Registrar	keeper of the records: student and academic
6.	Dean	head of "school"
7.	Academic Department Head	manager of academic department
8.	Director	manager of academic or other department or function
9.	Coordinator	organizer of function
10.	Professor	fully tenured and fully promoted
11.	Instructor	has expertise in field, non tenured (visiting or continuous visiting)
12.	Administrator	carries out a function (can be faculty or not; ex: dean is faculty and administrator
13.	Counselor	one who assists students in determining ways of solving problems or deliberates situations at the students' request
14.	Advisor	assists students in planning academic future

COMMONLY USED TERMS

15.	Academic Freedom	ability to teach and learn without fear of reprisal
16.	Academic integrity	scholarly honesty in research, publication, use of facilities and services, and the use of one's rank
17.	Billing hour	number of school hours that are billed for tuition (can include non-credit courses/0 level courses)
18.	Credit hour	number of hours in class and number of credits applicable to graduation
19.	Bingo sheet/plan of study	list of courses needed to complete a specific academic program (certificate, degree)
20.	Catalog	book of university rules, regulations, departments with course descriptions, faculty members' names and schooling history
21.	Experiential Learning	learning that takes place out of the normal classroom setting with the supervision of an instructor. Examples include but are not limited to internships, cooperative education, service learning, volunteer experiences.

22.	Internship	an arrangement whereby a student can gain experience in a company or agency involved in the work associated with the student's area of study (usually not paid)
23.	Full time/part time	12 credits or billable hours or more/under 12 hours
24.	PCSTAR	<u>P</u>urdue <u>C</u>alumet <u>ST</u>udent <u>A</u>ccess to <u>R</u>ecords
25.	Plagiarism	to use another's work and pass it off as your own
26.	Register (priority, open & late)	actually sign up for classes
27.	Schedule (noun & verb)	n. book of classes offered during a certain term. v. select classes for a certain term
28.	Syllabus	course outline of main points
29.	Student classification	(freshman, sophomore, junior, senior) based on number of credit hours completed that are applicable to declared degree. (see catalogue for breakdown)
30.	Tuition	fees charged for classes
31.	Resident	a student who lives within the borders of Indiana for a defined period of time and who pays Indiana income taxes or is the dependent of someone who does
32.	Non-resident	a student who has not lived within the borders of Indiana for a defined period of time and who does not pay Indiana income taxes or is not the dependent of someone who does
33.	Laboratory fee	fee charged students beyond tuition in order to provide students with laboratories required for certain courses
34.	Technology fee	fee charged students beyond tuition in order to provide students with the most up to date technology
35.	Student services fee	fee charged students beyond tuition in order to provide various services
36.	Admitted	given access to attend the university
37.	Prerequisite	course/s completed successfully *prior* to taking another course
38.	Corequisite	course/s to be taken simultaneously with another course
39.	Elective	choice of course open to student (free elective, any college course; major elective, any course from the student's primary area of study)
40.	General education	specific areas of study considered necessary to be educated
41.	Major	primary area of study
42.	Minor	secondary area of study
43.	Concentration/Option	specific courses that are meant to give added expertise
44.	Distance learning	learning outside of the classroom usually thru computer or satellite delivery of the course work
45.	Supplemental Instruction	process by which a fellow student assists students in traditionally difficult classes in order to grasp the material better. The supplemental instructor has already passed the course with high grades and works with the instructor in order to improve classroom learning.

46.	Tutoring	individual/small group assistance with a subject area that is challenging the student's understanding of it
47.	Writing Lab	service available to students who need assistance in writing papers or other writing homework
48.	Commencement	ceremony celebrating graduation, conferring of degrees, "beginning"
49.	CODO	Change Of Degree Objective: process by which a student changes his/her major. Permission to enter the major is granted by the new major department if the student meets minimum requirements set by that department.

GRADES AND ACADEMIC STUDENT STATUS

50.	GPA (grade point average/ graduation index)	overall average of all grades received
51.	Semester index	grade point average for the current semester
52.	Withdrawal	"drop" to remove a student from a class (can be done by the student or by the administration)
53.	Incomplete	grade stating that the student did not complete the course but will within a prescribed period of time after the term in which registered. This arrangement must be made with permission of the instructor only if the student is currently passing the course and has a valid reason for not completing the course within the original term.
54.	Satisfactory	grade stating that the student satisfied the requirements of a course
55.	Unsatisfactory	grade stating the student did not satisfy the requirements of a course
56.	Pass/fail	grading system by which no letter grade is given, only whether course was completed successfully or not
57.	Non-credit	course that does not bare university credit (usually remedial in nature)
58.	Audit	arrangement whereby a person can sit in on a class without earning credit
59.	Credit thru non-traditional means	testing out, AP credit, experiential credit
60.	Probation	warning period of time for poor academic performance or other reason
61.	Academic dismissal/drop	revocation of status as a student for poor academic performance
62.	Readmit	process of requesting admission after being dismissed/dropped
63.	Re-entry	process of returning to school after being away for a specific period of time (2 years at PUC)
64.	Other probations and dismissals	social, academic dishonesty, criminal activity, etc.
65.	Appeal	process by which a decision can be reviewed for reconsideration. Time limits usually exist for this process.
66.	Degree seeking	student who intends to earn a degree at this institution

67.	Non-degree seeking	student who intends to take courses without earning a degree
68.	Transfer	student who has attended college or university and has gained admission to another with the intent of earning a degree at the new institution
69.	Drop/add	process of changing one's schedule of classes

HIGHER EDUCATION'S INSTITUTIONAL LEVELS AND DEGREES

70.	Junior College	academic institution offering certification and associates degrees (aka "community college")
71.	College	one of the educational institutions within a university offering degrees in specific areas of study (sometimes called a "School" as in School of Management)
72.	Graduate school	advanced learning beyond a bachelor's degree
73.	University	educational institution for higher instruction that joins several colleges or schools and several more advanced and specialized faculties
74.	Graduate student	a student who has received a bachelor's degree and who is attending an institution of advanced learning
75.	Undergraduate student	a student who has not yet earned a bachelor's degree who is attending college
76.	Degree	academic rank or title conferred by an educational institution
77.	Associate of Arts	academic degree earned after completing 60+ credits in a specific subject area within the liberal arts
78.	Associate of Science	academic degree earned after completing 60+ credits in a specific subject area within the sciences or technology (applied)
79.	Bachelor of Arts	academic degree earned after completing 122+ credits in a specific area of study within the liberal arts
80.	Bachelor of Science	academic degree earned after completing 122+ credits in a specific area of study within the sciences or technology (applied)
81.	Master of Arts	advanced degree received upon completion of graduate program of study in the liberal arts
82.	Master of Science	advanced degree received upon completion of graduate program of study in the sciences or technology (applied)
83.	Ph.D.	("Doctor of Philosophy") advanced degree received upon completion of graduate plan of study that emphasizes research and investigation
84.	Certificate	recognition of completion of courses that can be useful to career or other activities

AREAS OF STUDY

85. **Aesthetics** — expressive "fine" arts such as painting, music, creative writing, etc. as opposed to "useful" arts

86. **Engineering** — designing and creating using science and math applied to the arts

87. **Lab Science** — science course with a laboratory experience

88. **Liberal Arts** — "arts suitable for free men"; study of literature, philosophy, language, history, etc. as opposed to "technical arts"

89. **Social Science** — any field of knowledge dealing with society (sociology, psychology, etc.)

90. **Technology** — application of designs to everyday uses

TERMS FOR TRANSFER STUDENTS

91. **Transfer credit** — courses that are acceptable to the new institution

92. **Undistributed credit** — courses that are not taught at new institution but may be usable in lieu of another course or as an elective

93. **Intercampus transfer** — moving to another Purdue campus

94. **Application for admission** — form to be completed and records that are requested in order to gain access to attend a college or university

2. Decoding Your Syllabus

DIRECTIONS: Using the *hardest or most important class you are taking this semester* as the subject of this exercise, take out all the materials for that course: syllabus, class schedule, any handouts that tell you what you will be doing in the course. Then answer the following questions.

Course Information: _____Department_____ Number _____ Section_____

1. Does this class require attendance? _____

2. How many absences if any are excused? _____

3. Do you know of any classes you definitely will miss? _____

4. What is the policy regarding missed exams, assignments, quizzes?

5. How are grades computed in this course?

   Judging by the way the grades are computed, on which parts of the course should you work the hardest?

6. What are the important dates in this course? List exam dates, due dates for assignments and when they are due.

   Is there a final exam? _____ Is it cumulative? _____

   Find the time and date for the final in the Schedule of Classes.

   Date _____ Time _____

7. What aspects of this course will cause the most trouble? Check all that apply.

Note taking   _____

Writing assignments   _____

Reading the text   _____

Speaking in front of the class   _____

Studying for exams   _____

Participating in class discussions   _____

Understanding basic concepts   _____

Other   _____ Explain.

8. Is this course required for your degree? _____

   Is there a minimum grade required for this class? _____

   What is the minimum grade? _____

   Is this class a prerequisite to another course you must take for your degree? _____

9. Is there anything in the syllabus that you do not understand? _____

   What is it?

   Where can you get help to understand?

10. Describe below your overall strategy for doing well in this course.

11. WHAT IS YOUR INSTRUCTOR'S NAME? _____
    (Memorize it!!!)

12. WHAT ARE THE INSTRUCTOR'S OFFICE HOURS? _____

3. Internet Search

1. Go to the PUC home page—*http://www.calumet.purdue.edu*

    Click on the section that indicates **SEARCH**. Be aware that there are many ways to find the different web pages requested. You need to use the technique that works best for you.

    When you click **SEARCH**, you will find a drop-down box called **SITE INDEX**.

    You can search for the various items there.

    *   Go to the **Registrar, Office of** web page and find the *Final Exam Schedule*. Print it.
    *   Go to the **Financial Aid & Student Accounts, Office of** web page and find the *Payment Plan Options* section. Print that page.
    *   Go to **PCSTAR** web page and access your *Current Schedule*. Print it.
    *   Go to **Center for Career Leadership & Development** found on the right hand side of the Office of Student Affairs web page under Quick Clicks. Print out the section on *Career Trax Student Login*.
    *   Go to the **Skills Assessment and Development Center** web page and find the section on *Tutoring*. Print it.
    *   Go to the **Center for Student Achievement** web page and find the "related links." Click on *Experiential Learning*. Read the information under each of the tabs at the top. Print the *FAQ information*.

2. STUDENT HANDBOOK QUESTIONS

    Go to the **Office of Student Affairs** web page and find *Quick Clicks* on the right hand side. Scroll down to and click on *"Publications."* Find **Student Handbook**. <u>Print *only* the page or part of page listed below</u>.

    *   Procedures of the Advising Process, the Responsibilities of the Advisor and the Advisee.
    *   The Attendance Policy
    *   Answer the following questions in your own words on a separate piece of paper following the guidelines listed in your syllabus for homework assignments
        *   What is the *Grade Appeals System* at PUC? How long do you have to appeal a grade?
        *   What does *Scholastic Drop* mean?
        *   What are two examples of misconduct listed in the Student Handbook under *Misconduct Subject to Disciplinary Penalties?*

3. QUESTIONS REGARDING THE SCHOOL THAT HOUSES YOUR MAJOR

    Go to your School's web page (ex: School of Liberal Arts, School of Management, etc.)

    Answer the following questions in your own words on the same sheet of paper used for Section 2 following the guidelines listed in your syllabus for homework assignments.

    *   What departments are in your School?
    *   What are the goals of your School?
    *   Who is the Dean of your School?
    *   Who are the academic advisors for your School or major department?

4. Plan of Study Assignment Instructions

This exercise is designed to teach the student how to plan out his/her academic program. The student will pick a major and select the courses to be taken for that degree. The courses for the plan are to be projected out 5 semesters. It is not necessary to know if the courses are actually offered. It is only necessary to list courses needed for the degree in the order they should be taken.

This assignment is worth **75 points**. Points are broken down into 15 points for each semester's plan. Please consider spending some time on this assignment to ensure that you receive as many of the 75 points as possible.

1. Top portion of the form—your choice of degree (Ex: BS in Management, BS in Accounting, BS in Computer Information Systems, BA in Business, BA in Sociology or BA in Psychology) *must match* your intended major!

2. First column—Subject and Course number—for example, **MGMT 200.**

3. Second column— # Credits—for example, **3** credits (for MGMT 200).

4. Third column—Pre-requisite #—you are to list the pre-requisite class. Example, **MA 153** (for MGMT 200, Psy 203).

5. Fourth Column—Course Title—**Introductory Accounting, Introduction to Psychology.**

6. Add up the total number of credit hours for each semester.

7. Where can you obtain the required information for columns 1–4?

   Answer! Course catalog and class schedule online, ask an advisor.

8. Attach a copy of the Plan of Study (bingo sheet) to this assignment.

HERE IS A SAMPLE:

NAME ____John Doe_____   BS OR BA _____BS Management_____

DATE _____2/14/09_____   INTENDED MAJOR _____Finance_____

Current Semester's courses ____Fall 2009____

SUBJ/CRSE #	# CREDIT/S	PRE-REQUISITE #	COURSE TITLE
Engl 104	3	SAT score or EPT	Engl Comp I
Mgmt 100	1	None	Mgmt Lectures
Soc 100	3	None	Intro to Sociology
Ma 021	0	MPT score	Beginning Algebra
Mgmt 101	3	None	Intro to Business
	10	TOTAL CREDIT HOURS FOR THIS SEMESTER	

9. Items for inclusion in the "Notes" section:

    a.   Summer classes Place * between spring & fall term where you plan to take course/s

    b.   Transfer credits Place * above the "Current semester" section

    c.   Classes taken previously to this semester Place * above the "Current semester" section

    d.   Placement test credit (ex. Foreign language or Math placement) Place * above the "Current semester" section

    e.   Advanced Placement test credit from high school Place * above the "Current semester" section

    f.   Dual credits from high school Place * above the "Current semester" section

    g.   CLEP credits Place * above the "Current semester" section

    h.   Any other special information pertinent to this assignment

    i.   If you are changing schools within PUC or transferring to another school, please attach your new plan of study (bingo sheet) to this assignment

10. **Please note: you cannot take a pre-requisite class in the same semester as the class that requires the pre-requisite** (for example, MA 153 and MGMT 200 cannot be taken in the same semester; you must take MA 153 in one semester and MGMT 200 or for Psych majors, PSY 203 in the next semester).

11. For the BS in Manage. Acct. degree, you should concentrate on taking your pre-management courses first before going on to upper (300+) level classes.

12. For the BA degree, you should concentrate on taking your pre-business courses first before going on to the rest of your courses.

13. Some classes may have a class restriction (OBHR 330 and MGMT 301 or PSY 480 and SOC 307). In these examples, you need to have a junior classification (Class 5 means at least 61 credit hours attained). You can add up the total number of credit hours earned per semester to see if you meet this requirement.

14. Any questions before turning in this assignment? Please ask your freshman course instructor.

15. **Hint:** It is easier to plan out the courses needed if the student has the "bingo sheet" or the list of degree requirements for the intended major.

5. Plan of Study

Name: _____   BS or BA _____

Date _____   Intended Major _____

Current Semester's Courses _____

SUBJ/CRSE #	# CREDIT/S	PRE-REQUISITE #	COURSE TITLE

	Total CREDIT Hours for this Semester

Semester 2 _____

SUBJ/CRSE #	# CREDIT/S	PRE-REQUISITE #	COURSE TITLE

	Total CREDIT Hours for this Semester

Semester 3 _____

SUBJ/CRSE #	# CREDIT/S	PRE-REQUISITE #	COURSE TITLE

	Total CREDIT Hours for this Semester

Semester 4 _____

SUBJ/CRSE #	# CREDIT/S	PRE-REQUISITE #	COURSE TITLE

| | Total CREDIT Hours for this Semester |

Semester 5 _____

SUBJ/CRSE #	# CREDIT/S	PRE-REQUISITE #	COURSE TITLE

| | Total CREDIT Hours for this Semester |

Notes: _____

_____

_____

_____

_____

_____

_____

_____

_____

_____

_____

6. Tips and Questions for the Interview for Information

Tips for conducting the Interview for Career Information:

- Select several persons who may be able to provide you with the time and who have the experience in the career you want to pursue.
- Call the person/s to make an appointment for about 1 hour. Inform him/her that the **purpose of your interview** is to complete a class assignment, **NOT** to apply for a job. Make sure you have your planner with you when you make the call so you have your availability in front of you.
- Be sure to allow the person you are interviewing to offer his/her availability first and then see if you can fit it into yours.
- Be sure to confirm your appointment the day before by calling the person or his/her secretary.
- On the day of the interview, dress appropriately. Dress professionally, as if you already held the job; or if not, then as neatly as you would for a special occasion.
- Be polite and defer to the person you are interviewing.
- Make sure to let the person know that you will be taking notes about what is said so that you can write your paper.
- You can ask all the questions listed below or those that seem appropriate. Let the person talk freely. He/she may give you more information than what is being asked. It can be more helpful in writing your paper if you use your active listening skills. Remember you are *seeking information only*.
- Be sure to shake hands and thank the person for his/her time and knowledge.
- Follow up with a thank you letter, in business format. Express how the person helped you.

Interview for Career Information Questions:

- What is a typical workday like in your job?
- What is the most rewarding part of this job?
- Is there company training necessary for the job? What does it entail?
- How would you describe the ideal candidate for an entry level job leading to your level? What talents are needed?
- How would you describe both the physical and psychological working environment?
- How does this job connect with the other people in this department? Team or individual work? How does it fit into the company as a whole?
- What are the possibilities for professional growth and advancement?
- What is the turnover like in this job? What is the average tenure of employees in this position? Do they move to another company or move to another position within?

- What part of the job is most challenging? Why?
- If you could, what would you change about your job? Why?
- What are the strengths that a person needs to do this job successfully?
- How much travel or overtime is expected? Is it constant, seasonal, or occasional?
- Is this career more analytical or more people oriented or both?
- How is performance feedback or review conducted? By whom and how often?

7. Final Portfolio Project

The idea of this project is to develop a comprehensive package that displays usable information about you as a person, your education plan, and your goals for the future. By pulling together some of the activities and homework assignments that you have completed during the semester, and doing some additional research into your career, you will have created your own roadmap. This portfolio is to be assembled in the following order in a folder that is clean and professional looking. Appearance and presentation counts.

PORTFOLIO CONTENTS

1. Title Page: Project Title; the course number/section; course title; instructor's name; student's name
2. Contents Page listing the Sections and their contents, including page numbers
3. Section 1: "It's All About Me"
   a. Essay (1 page minimum) on who I am now versus who I was on the first day of college. What have I learned about myself?
   b. Homework: Learning Styles Assignment
4. Section 2: My Educational Plan
   a. Homework: Plan of Study Assignment
   b. Copy of upcoming semester's class registration
5. Section 3: My Future
   a. Essay on "Why I selected this career" (1 page minimum) to include:
      i. Your plan to reach your career goal stating experiential learning opportunities available or part time work that will enhance your opportunities; also list degrees and training necessary
      ii. Current information regarding job prospects and *entry level salaries* for this career.
   b. Homework: Career Research Assignment
   c. Interview for Information with a person who is *currently in your chosen career.* (2 pages minimum.) Include the person's name, title, company name and address, at the beginning of the essay.
   d. Homework: Two Persons to Interview
   e. Copy of the thank you letter in business format that you sent to the person you interviewed
6. Section 4: Sources
   Be sure to cite any outside sources you have used in gathering your materials for this portfolio. A bibliography of publications and/or websites is needed as well as the names, titles, company names and addresses for the persons used for interviews or other information. A minimum of three sources must be cited. APA format for the citations is preferred.

8. The Drawbridge Exercise

DIRECTIONS: Please read the story completely. Then follow the instructions.

As he left for a visit to his outlying districts, the jealous Baron warned his pretty wife: "Do not leave the castle while I am gone, or I will punish you severely when I return!"

But as the hours passed the young Baroness grew lonely, and despite her husband's warning, decided to visit her lover who lived in the countryside nearby.

The castle was located on an island in a wide, fast flowing river, with a drawbridge linking the island on the land at the narrowest point in the river.

"Surely my husband will not return before dawn," she thought, and ordered her servants to lower the drawbridge and leave it down until she returned.

After spending several pleasant hours with her lover, the Baroness returned to the drawbridge, only to find it blocked by a madman wildly waving a long and crude knife.

"Do not attempt to cross this bridge, Baroness, or I will kill you," he raved.

Fearing for her life, the Baroness returned to her lover and asked him to help.

"Our relationship is only a romantic one," he said, "I will not help."

The Baroness then sought out a boatman on the river, explained her plight to him and asked him to take her across the river in his boat.

"I will do it, but only if you can pay my fee of five Marks."

"But I have no money with me!" the Baroness protested.

"That is too bad. No money, no ride," the boatman said flatly.

Her fear growing, the Baroness ran crying to the home of a friend, and after again explaining the situation, begged for enough money to pay the boatman his fee.

"If you had not disobeyed your husband, this would not have happened," the friend said. "I will give you no money."

With dawn approaching and her last resource exhausted, the Baroness returned to the bridge in desperation, attempted to cross to the castle and was slain by the madman.

DIRECTIONS: In the story there are six characters. They are (in alphabetical order):

The Baron _____   The Friend _____

The Baroness _____   The Lover _____

The Boatman _____   The Madman _____

Using the list above, rank the characters 1 through 6 in the order of their responsibility for the death of the Baroness. The rank of "1" holds the most responsibility.

Now, work with the other members of your group and decide on a **group** rank order for the six characters.

9. Grades, GPAs, Academic Honors

Students must complete all required work for courses by the last scheduled class. The only exception is if the course has been cancelled. At the end of each semester, students will receive a grade from the instructor for each course they enroll in. The grade indicates the level of achievement of the objectives of the course. Grades offered at Purdue Calumet are listed below. Please note that beginning with the Fall 2008 semester, the plus/minus grade option (B+/B/B-) will be available for assignment at the instructor's discretion.

THE FOLLOWING GRADING SCALE WILL BE USED:

A+, A	94–100%
A–	90–93%
B+	87–89%
B	84–86%
B–	80–83%
C+	77–79%
C	74–76%
C–	70–73%
D+	67–69%
D	64–66%
D–	60–63%
F	Below 60%

CALCULATING THE GPA:

The general formula for calculating a GPA is the weighted grade X semester hours = index points. The sum of all the index points divided by the number of semester hours is the GPA. A semester index GPA is an average of all of the index points for that semester; a cumulative GPA is an average of all of index points that the student has received

For the purpose of averaging, each grade shall be weighted and index points calculated as indicated.

Grade	Weight
A+, A	4.0 × semester hrs = index pts
A–	3.7 × semester hrs = index pts
B+	3.3 × semester hrs = index pts
B	3.0 × semester hrs = index pts
B–	2.7 × semester hrs = index pts
C+	2.3 × semester hrs = index pts
C	2.0 × semester hrs = index pts
C–	1.7 × semester hrs = index pts

D+	1.3 × semester hrs = index pts
D	1.0 × semester hrs = index pts
D–	0.7 × semester hrs = index pts
E,F,WF,EF,IF	0.0 × semester hrs = index pts
P,N,I,PI,SI,W	*Not included in GPA calculation*
WN,WU,IN,IU	*Not included in GPA calculation*

ACADEMIC HONORS

Dean's List: Each semester the Dean's List honors undergraduate students who have at least 12 credit hours in the graduation index with a graduate index of at least 3.5, and have at least six hours in the semester index of at least 3.0.

Students whose names are placed on the Dean's List shall be entitled to the following special privileges during the semester following the designation of distinction:

- May be assigned to more than 18 credit hours upon request.
- With the instructor's permission, a full-time Dean's List student may audit one class with assessment or additional fee.

Semester Honors: Semester Honors recognize undergraduate students who:

- Have at least six credit hours in the semester index with a semester index of at least 3.5 and
- Have at least a 2.0 graduation index.

If would be possible to earn both Dean's List and Semester Honors standing if the student has a really outstanding semester.

Note: Pass/no pass grades and credits in hour totals for either category of honors.

Sources: Academic Catalog, 2008–2009, pages 22 and 25; Plus/Minus grades information from a memo from VC for Academic Affairs dated 12/9/08.

10. Financial Aid & Academic Progress

OFFICE OF FINANCIAL AID AND STUDENT ACCOUNTS

Satisfactory Academic Progress Policy

Financial Aid recipients must be making Satisfactory Academic Progress toward a degree objective in order to be eligible to receive financial aid through Purdue University Calumet. The Satisfactory Academic Progress Policy at Purdue University Calumet is based on standards established by Federal Regulations governing student financial aid. These standards are cumulative and include all periods of a student's enrollment, including periods in which the student did not receive student financial aid.

Students are considered to be meeting the Satisfactory Academic Progress standards if the following three (3) requirements (standards) are met:

1. **GPA Requirement.** Undergraduate students whose attempted credit hours are greater than 24 credit hours must maintain a minimum graduation index based on their current grade classification as outlined below. Graduate students whose attempted credit hours are greater than 15 credit hours must maintain a minimum graduation index of 3.00.

Current Grade Classification	Minimum Required Graduation Index
1	1.50
2	1.60
3	1.70
4	1.80
5	1.90
6	2.00
7	2.00
8	2.00
M or B	3.00

2. **Completion Rate Requirement.** In order to show progression toward completion of their program of study, a student's overall total number of **earned** (completed) credit hours must be equal to or greater than 67% of the overall total number of their **attempted** credit hours.

Student is meeting the Completion Rate Requirement if:

Overall Earned Credit Hours >= 67% of Overall Attempted Credit Hours

Example: Student's Overall Earned Credit Hours is 127
Student's Overall Attempted Credit Hours of 136

136 x .67 = 91 (minimum number of Overall Earned Credit Hours the student must have)

As the Student's Overall Earned Credit Hours (127) is greater than 67% of the Students Overall

Attempted Credit Hours (136 x .67 or 91), the student is meeting the Completion Rate Requirement.

3. **Timeframe.** The average length of an undergraduate program of study at Purdue University Calumet is 126 credit hours. An undergraduate student is eligible to receive financial aid for a maximum of 189 attempted credit hours at Purdue University Calumet. **Graduate students** may receive financial aid for a maximum of 90 attempted credit hours.

(over)

Plan for success with Purdue University Calumet

General Information:

- **Transfer credit hours are included in determining attempted credit hours.**
- **Withdrawals, grades of "incomplete", courses that are repeated, and non-credit courses are included in determining a student's Satisfactory Academic Progress status.**

Probationary Status:

Students failing to meet the GPA or Completion Rate requirements as outlined are placed on Financial Aid Probation for one semester. While on Financial Aid Probation the student is eligible to receive student financial aid. Students failing to meet the GPA or Completion Rate requirements by the end of their Probationary period automatically become ineligible to receive financial aid and remain ineligible until they again are meeting all the Satisfactory Academic Progress requirements.

Ineligible Status:

Students in an ineligible status are not eligible to receive student financial aid at Purdue University Calumet. A student's eligibility for financial aid will automatically be reinstated once they again meet the GPA **and** Completion Rate requirements*. **Note:** Students who fail to complete any of their attempted credit hours during any one semester or session automatically become ineligible to receive financial aid for one semester. Their eligibility will be reinstated after one semester as long as they are meeting the GPA and Completion Rate requirements.

*Students, who become ineligible due to timeframe cannot have their financial aid reinstated even if they are meeting the other Satisfactory Academic Progress requirements.

Appeal Process:

An ineligible status (except in the case where a student is ineligible due to no longer meeting the timeframe requirement) can be appealed if the student has had mitigating circumstances such as personal illness or injury, or the death of an immediate family member. Students may obtain a copy of the appeal form by accessing http://www.calumet.purdue.edu/finaid/SAPAPPEAL.pdf or by contacting the Office of Financial Aid and Student Accounts to request a Satisfactory Academic Progress Appeal form. Note: A probationary status cannot be appealed.

Students submitting an appeal form will be contacted through their Purdue University Calumet assigned web assigned as to the status of their appeal.

Payment after Reinstatement:

A student may be paid Pell Grant and campus-based funds, state funds, and/or Direct Student Loan funds for the payment period in which the student is again meeting Satisfactory Academic Progress standards, but cannot be paid for any payment period during which time the student was in an ineligible status.